ENDORSEMENTS

Wendy Alec's understanding of the Father God's heart to a simple child of His and a princess is quite simply beyond comparison to anything I've ever read.

As I ingested each word, I was taken into gardens, meadows, a chamber, and the personal presence of the Almighty. The visions and theophanies are quite honestly life changing.

Her personal pain and suffering, while designing a model script for the marketplace, arrested the attention of every demon from hell and drew them to this innocent soul, Wendy Alec. This book has no resting place. Indeed, I was kept attentive throughout every page because it relates to our everyday suffering and pain, while seeking an answer from our Father God. He showed Wendy the power of patience and standing still and waiting.

This book ministered to me personally and gave me the understanding of how to personally deal with our sufferings. There is an answer in the midst of every trial. But you have to press forward . . . not backwards.

Wendy, thank you. I'm another man because of your book *Visions from Heaven*.

Kim Clement – *Kim Clement Ministries*

Wendy Alec is, without a doubt, one of the most gifted seers I know. She is destined to bring a spiritual revolution to media of all kinds.

If you are in the midst of a deep and dark season and you do not think you will ever come out on the other side, this book is for you!

Wendy has gone through such a time, faced despair and survived with joy! Her *Visions from Heaven* will help pull you out of the pit of sorrow into God's promise of abundant life.

Cindy Jacobs – *Co-founder, Generals International*

Wendy Alec's *Visions from Heaven: Visitations to My Father's Chamber* is perhaps the most important Christian book to be released in recent history. Whether the reader has gone through a crippling and traumatic disease or an epic betrayal and rejection by other Believers who just "didn't know what they were doing," this book was written just for you—personally! And if you've ever wondered what was on God's heart when He allowed you to be found in your awful situation, family or marriage, then this is what you must read today! If you are unsure if your loved one, once a devoted Christian, seemed to lose his faith toward the end of his life—was even saved at his passing—then buy *Visions from Heaven*.

And finally, if you've struggled in your own life, wondering where God is when you are hurting deeply and He remains so very silent, pick up this book and don't put it down until you've read it cover to cover! This work is so important that it should be required reading at every Christian Academy and Bible College around the world. And each Theological Seminary and every Church ministry training center should require its reading by every ministerial and missions trainee. This book is THAT IMPORTANT. This truly is an amazing book, and it answered MANY of my own hard questions for God!

Steve Shultz – *Founder and Publisher, Elijah List*

Wendy Alec has done it again! Rarely do we find such a combination of scriptural content, prophetic edge, and poetic capacity in writing converged in one person to create a work of art. In *Visions from Heaven: Visitations to My Father's Chamber*, we have a book that is inspirational and yet solid as a rock! Read and be touched by Our Father in Jesus' name!

James W. Goll – *Director of Encounters Network and Prayer Storm*

In my life and ministry around the world I am witnessing the greatest positioning in all industries of mature believers into the fullness of what God has made for them, but before they are positioned and placed, many have been so beat down and attacked that it takes an encounter like Wendy's to bring the understanding that is necessary to come back from hope deferred or disappointment.

So many times while reading this book I pictured friends, colleagues, family members who need the revelation in this book. I felt like I was changing, like the encounter was mine not just Wendy's.

Visions from Heaven reappoints faith in the fullness of who God is.

I have never read anything quite like it and I know so many amazing believers who are even leaders in church, business, the entertainment industry, or in other areas who need to read this perspective because it actually draws a line in the sand of the heart from which there is no coming back. You are confronted with the love of God, with the plan of Heaven, and with the

thoughts of the Father, and I believe this book will detoxify people from spiritually intense seasons and help to restore spiritual clarity and health. Please read this book!
Shawn Bolz – *Senior Pastor of Expression58*

Like Wendy, I have suffered much on so many occasions. I too have been told there is no hope just like Wendy was. There in the valley of the shadow of death with no real answers. With no real answer from the Church and with no instant healing and total despair. Wendy does not descend further into the mire of total despair. She was low, so low and there already. She ascends to the highest heavens and there she sits with our Lord, the Creator of the universe. There she tells a story like no other I have ever heard; there she takes you, the reader, to the heavens with her.

This is a book like no other, whatever your despair. As you go with Wendy into this inspirational, prophetic book, you to will enter into the heavens. You, too, like me in the middle of the war in Baghdad, can move into the throne room of the Almighty and, like Wendy, see the glory of the Lord and find His healing, His wholeness and His love. This book is a must.
The Rev'd Canon Dr. Andrew White – *Vicar of Baghdad*

In *Visions from Heaven: Visitations to My Father's Chamber*, Wendy Alec beautifully scribes her heavenly encounters that offer impartations of courage, faith, comfort, and perseverance to those going through seasons of intense personal trial and devastations. With great candor and vulnerability she shares her own personal journey – its pain, fears, questions, doubts and even her sense of abandonment in the midst of her darkest hours. This book is truly a message from the Father's heart. He has prayed that your faith may not fail you in the midst of your journey. The Victor's crown is awaiting you who have persevered. If you don't quit, you win! Wendy did not quit. Wendy won. So will you!
Patricia King – *Co-founder of xpmedia.com Inc.*

Have you ever felt that you're experiencing the life of Job because no matter where you turn there's yet another test, trial or temptation? There's no escape clause in this game of life and you must hold on to the only hope you can find. And this hope is the intimate fellowship with the Father. In these heartfelt pages of *Visions from Heaven: Visitations to My Father's Chamber* you'll witness Wendy's courageous battle through a Job-like experience. And you'll learn how to endure these tests for a divine purpose in Christ and come through them victoriously. Many who have gone through these tests are being approved to come forth in a new anointing for the harvest.

I highly recommend this book to the overcomer.

Bob Jones – *Bob Jones Ministries*

Wendy Alec's powerful book, *Visions from Heaven: Visitations to My Father's Chamber*, is the story of redemption and restoration out of Wendy's excruciating physical and emotional pain. *Visions from Heaven* offers a lifeline to those drowning in a sea of hopelessness and depression. If you or someone you love is questioning God in the midst of a trial, this book will be a beacon of hope in an ocean of despair. I highly recommend this book!

Kris Vallotton – *Senior Associate Leader, Bethel Church, Redding, CA*

I read *Visions from Heaven* with a vast framework of emotions, from joy to quiet tears. This is a great book for anyone wanting insight into the realm of God's heart for His people, from new beginners in their walk to the seasoned warrior.

Wow, what an awesome insight into the inner workings of the Lord's heart.

Ian Clayton – *Sons of Thunder, New Zealand*

Wendy Alec has always been a transparent vessel and voice for Kingdom authority, power, and glory. She has a sensitivity to the Spirit that is both admirable and worthy of emulation. Wendy, too, went through a strange and fiery ordeal. What I find so marvelous is the way God has taken that pain she endured and turned it into a promise for all of us as we prepare for the next great awakening that is going to touch this planet.

Wendy's writing is seamless, and she takes us through a series of portals into vistas of the Father's great and loving purpose for His children and for the Kingdom in these great days. I applaud her for her courage to be a voice that is willing to be heard because many will not only find hope; they will find courage, and healing, and ultimately wholeness.

If ever you needed encouragement, *Visions from Heaven*, will provide it.

Dr. Mark Chironna – *Church On The Living Edge – Mark Chironna Ministries*

VISIONS *from* HEAVEN

Wendy Alec

VISITATIONS TO MY FATHER'S CHAMBER

WARBOYS PUBLISHING

Published by Warboys Publishing (Ireland) Limited
77 Sir John Rogerson's Quay, Dublin 2, Ireland

ISBN: 978-0-9928063-0-9

Cover design by W. Alec, C. Bown and Studiogearbox
Typeset by CRB Associates, Potterhanworth, Lincolnshire, UK
Printed in the United States of America

CONTENTS

FOREWORD

I wasn't sure what to expect when I began reading Wendy Alec's book, *Visions from Heaven: Visitations to My Father's Chamber*. I knew about her terrible difficulties with her rare illness and recovery, but nothing prepared me for her deep feelings of God's abandonment and her journey out of those life-and-death struggles.

From the first pages of her introduction, brought alive with the most vivid, firsthand descriptions, she shares her most intimate times with God in which she was eventually allowed to see the throne room, the meadow, and the Father's chamber. What she unveils in each place will forever change your perceptions of God's kingdom; and her breathtaking descriptions of Heaven that will cause you to long for our eternal home.

She was given two birthday gifts by the Lord: One was a large aquamarine box tied with a beautiful pale pink bow and diamonds glistening from the center of the bow, deeply meaningful beyond words. The second gift was a fountain pen flowing with blood and fire with these instructions: "Tell My children how I yearn for them, how I long for their fellowship, that I will never, never abandon them."

Blood and fire from that pen explode on every page of this amazing book. *Visions from Heaven* reads with the allegorical drama of a C. S. Lewis masterpiece and is power-packed with words of revelation, caution, and encouragement flowing directly from God's heart to Wendy and all of His children everywhere!

There's not enough room in this foreword to describe all my favorite passages – the Scottish girl, the discouraged pastor, the missionaries who toiled for years in China, the evangelist attacked by the enemy in unspeakable ways. Instead, let me tell you that this book is profoundly life changing, astonishingly eye opening, and deeply heartrending. It was birthed with many tears and will cause you to weep again and again.

If you are facing discouragement, adversity, disillusionment, afflictions, physical sickness, bereavement, loss, heartbreak, feeling of abandonment by God Himself, this book will lift you, give you hope, and build your faith in the most remarkable way!

Pastor Benny Hinn
Founder Benny Hinn Ministries

FOREWORD

Reading *Visions from Heaven: Visitations to My Father's Chamber* was both a wonderful and challenging experience. Wonderful because it invites us to experience the author's magnificent encounters with God. Challenging because it addresses so many difficult subjects. Wendy Alec accomplishes both goals with beauty and grace.

Contained in these pages is arguably the most important revelation one could ever receive – the nature of our heavenly Father. This also happens to be the primary revelation that Jesus came to give us, as the Gospel of John makes quite clear. With that value in mind, Wendy reveals God's Father heart brilliantly by bringing us into her personal walk with Him, revealed in part through her Father–daughter conversations.

I am thankful that the idea of God being our good and wonderful Father has taken center stage in recent years. The number of books on the subject has been increasing quite regularly. And rightly so. They address a profound need that exists in most of our lives. Unfortunately, this concept often remains just a teaching or discussion topic. All too seldom is this concept seen as an experience from which people can draw for the rest of their days. Unfortunately, it often remains just a doctrine or idea that gives intellectual comfort as we process the affairs of daily life.

What Wendy Alec brings us is different. These words are not mere ideas taken from a book. Nor are they lofty statements spoken to flatter us or give us false hopes. Not at all. The material offered to us in this book was obtained in the *dark night of the soul*. These insights came directly from the Throne Room to this treasured daughter of God. Much of what you'll read is actual Father–daughter dialogue. It is always honest, sometimes painful, and eternally triumphant. I'm so glad the Father has given her permission to share this with us, as this is private and personal, but filled with promise.

Miracles are an extremely important part of the gospel and are, therefore, to be a vital part of the life of a believer. However, the miracle spoken of in this book is rarely taught, and even more rarely understood. It is a miracle that came from process. If we are honest, most of us would admit that our favorite miracle is the instant miracle. That's where the tumor dissolves before our eyes, or the deaf ears are instantly opened, or the miracle of provision comes almost like manna on the ground. These are the kinds of things I've been able to enjoy more and more in recent years. Yet miracles of process are still supernatural gifts of God. Tragically, many believers abort their own miracle because of ignorance in this subject. *Visions from Heaven* will be used to answer that need in a very powerful way.

This transparent look into Wendy Alec's life is a look into process, her process into the miracle that saved her life. I am certain that understanding this process through Wendy's testimony will save countless lives.

Wendy Alec stands as a watchman on the wall. She has written quite openly about the struggles and pains of walking through affliction into her miracle. Yet, as powerful as Wendy's story is, this book is equally powerful in announcing what is coming. She stands tall, proclaiming to us what is about to happen in the Church, and, therefore, in the world. We are coming into the most thrilling season any of us has ever experienced before. I believe Wendy is completely accurate as she declares the nature of the days directly ahead. *Visions from Heaven* contains an important prophetic decree of where God is taking us. I am thrilled that this book is now available to the people of God!

Bill Johnson
Senior Leader of Bethel Church, Redding, CA
Author of *When Heaven Invades Earth* and *Hosting the Presence*

GREAT IS THY FAITHFULNESS,
O GOD MY FATHER,
THERE IS NO SHADOW OF TURNING WITH THEE;
THOU CHANGEST NOT,
THY COMPASSIONS, THEY FAIL NOT;
AS THOU HAST BEEN
THOU FOREVER WILT BE.

GREAT IS THY FAITHFULNESS!
GREAT IS THY FAITHFULNESS!
MORNING BY MORNING
NEW MERCIES I SEE;
ALL I HAVE NEEDED
THY HAND HATH PROVIDED,
GREAT IS THY FAITHFULNESS,
LORD, UNTO ME!

PARDON FOR SIN AND A PEACE THAT ENDURETH,
THINE OWN DEAR PRESENCE TO CHEER AND TO GUIDE;
STRENGTH FOR TODAY AND BRIGHT HOPE FOR TOMORROW,
BLESSINGS ALL MINE, WITH TEN THOUSAND BESIDES.

Thomas Obadiah Chisholm (1866–1960) © Hope Publishing Co.

As a father loves *and* pities his children,
so the Lord loves *and* pities those who fear Him
[with reverence, worship, and awe].

For He knows our frame,
He [earnestly] remembers *and* imprints
[on His heart] that we are dust.

(Psalm 103:13–14)

INTRODUCTION

FOR THOSE WALKING THROUGH THE VALLEY OF THE SHADOW

Beloved friend,

As I was writing this introduction, I felt the Holy Spirit say, "Even as *this* book has been forged by tears . . . there are many of My sons and My daughters whose past season has also been forged in tears, in agony of soul and in endurance. But even as I delivered My people, Israel, from Pharaoh and out of Egypt – I am about to deliver My people from the wilderness and from a season of adversity into a *'brand-new day.'*"

Beloved, if this is you – if you have recently been through a season of severe adversity and testing and found yourself at the sheer rock face, facing some of the fiercest trials and testing of your life head on, I believe with all my heart that it is no coincidence you are reading these pages, but that the Father Himself loves you so intensely, that He has done everything He can to put this book into your hands.

Maybe you or those you love have experienced a crippling bereavement . . .

The loss of a loved one that you felt was before their time.

Maybe you have experienced chronic sickness . . .

The loss of a beloved child or babe in arms . . .

Maybe you have experienced a heartbreaking abandonment by your husband or wife . . .

The loss of your family home or your business . . .

A devastating financial loss . . .

And yet you have loved the Father, the Lord Jesus and His Holy Spirit with all your heart and soul.

You have served Him these past years to the very best of your ability.

And so, secretly, your heart has been breaking with bewilderment and abandonment.

Not only over the agonies of these trials.

But because Heaven itself has seemed silent.

So silent.

And so, in the midnight hour, when it is only you and God, your pillow has been soaked with tears of desperation from unanswered questions . . . and from your abandoned heart.

In our greatest seasons of adversity, Satan tries to imprint his own character onto our Father's faultless, flawless one.

And in the searing heat of our battle, this sometimes outworks itself in his accusations to our souls to accuse our own omniscient Father in our minds and hearts.

Oh, greatly beloved, it is my heartfelt hope that, within these pages, you will find rest, peace and hope.

Knowing that the Great Sifting is now over.

Knowing that whether you have been in a season of sifting, of intense warfare or a season when you were caught off guard and your own momentary vulnerabilities and unhealed wounds were a landing ground for the enemy.

That you will find such tender answers from our incredible Father – the Father of *all* compassion and pity.

That through the visions from the Throne Room in these pages, you will gain new strength to rise up again to a new day.

A new season.

And that *His* Glory and *His* Power and *His* Kingdom – the favor and unfathomable love and mercies and compassions of the Father Himself will wrap around your physical body, your mind and your soul like a mantle.

For it is HE.

The Faithful One.

The Kindest and most tender One of all.

The very Balm of Gilead Himself, who reaches out His arms toward you today.

Tenderly entreating you out of abandonment

And bids you . . .

. . . Come . . .

BLESSED BE THE GOD AND FATHER OF OUR LORD JESUS CHRIST, THE FATHER OF SYMPATHY (PITY AND MERCY) AND THE GOD [WHO IS THE SOURCE] OF EVERY COMFORT (CONSOLATION AND ENCOURAGEMENT).
(2 Corinthians 1:3)

VOLUME ONE

THE VALLEY OF THE SHADOW

How would I ever feel safe again?

It was finally over.

Ninety percent of the agony and physical suffering of the past twenty-four months was now behind me.

My healing had finally manifested.

But the grueling physical and mental trauma of the 'fight' had left its scars.

After months of experiencing what I can only describe as feeling totally 'abandoned' by the magnificent God who I had known nearly my entire Christian life as my most beautiful, compassionate Heavenly Father.

The Father of Lights.

The great Father of mercies.

The God of such kindness and compassion.

I was now standing profoundly shaken . . . but still standing,

On the very edge, about to step out of the searing, flaming wilderness.

But I had literally been shaken to the core of my very being.

Unless I was able to find the answers, it was very probable that I would never be able to feel completely safe again.

I only had two options that lay before me.

To live the rest of my life in a whirlwind of trauma and unanswered questions or to step from the searing wilderness into the Throne Room . . . .

A VISIT TO MY FATHER'S CHAMBER

*I*t was my birthday.

It was actually my fifty-third birthday.

I was in Jerusalem, Israel, filming for TV.

Now – two years later – my physical body was already in a restoration process and I wanted to spend my birthday with my Heavenly Father.

We'd had a long day of filming in our TV studios and it must have been around two in the morning, the time when often I am with 'Daddy.'

Lately, my visits with 'Daddy' had taken place in three distinct places.

I would find myself in the Throne Room, in a vast meadow, or in what seemed to be one of the Father's chambers, which seemed like an intimate library.

Whenever I visit him in *this* chamber, I call it 'My Father's Chamber.'

I find myself sitting on His lap and I seem to be snuggling into His chest.

In front of us is a huge desk; sometimes it appears to be an altar of some kind.

Many times when I am there, there is a large open book on the table in front of us, which He explained to me is my personal Book of Life, and from which He often explains many things to me.

I never see much further into the rest of the Chamber.

One particular visit, I had picked bunches of flowers for my beautiful Heavenly Father and one bunch of roses that I had given Him instantly became embedded in the left-hand wall of this chamber – it was incredible – they were living, breathing flowers decorating His wall – like living floral wallpaper. Exquisite, beautiful.

The second place where I have found myself often recently is THE MEADOW.

It is a vast, brightly green meadow filled with the most incredible array of flowers.

To my far left, far off, is my earthly father's own garden. My earthly father is often painting using an easel. Sometimes he is playing the violin.

To my far right is the Heavenly Father's own personal rose garden. Oh, how incredible!

He walks in His heavenly garden like He used to walk with Adam and Eve and watches as I play in the meadow.

But today, on my birthday, I found myself in 'My Father's Chamber.'

I had such an excitement in my spirit as I visited Him this evening.

Sometimes when I visit Him there, I seem to be a small child of around four or five, but today I felt I was around nineteen, it seemed – a princess coming of age.

"Daddy, Daddy! It's my birthday!" I cuddled into Him.

I was excited – for I knew somehow that my Daddy had a gift for me.

I was right. There, on the table in front of us, was a large box, beautifully wrapped in the palest aquamarine, my favorite color in the entire world, and it had a beautiful, pale pink bow around it. Diamonds glistened from the center of the bow.

"Unwrap it." I could literally hear that gorgeous 'twinkle' in His voice.

I slid off His lap.

Suddenly, I was standing on the far side of His chamber and walking towards Him – walking through the thick, thick presence of His glory.

Saturated in His presence.

Hardly able to walk toward Him because of the sheer weight of the Glory that emanated from Him.

With one foot before the other, I walked towards His table.

I carefully untied the pink bow and then removed the wrapping.

I lifted the lid and gasped.

Inside the box, in beautiful pale aqua tissue paper, lay the most exquisite tiara.

It was silver, with diamonds and pale aquamarine stones.

I lifted it up with both hands and carefully slipped it on my head, but something hard seemed to be in the way.

Softly, I ran my fingers over small fragments of glass protruding from my head.

I gasped in shock, looking back to my Father.

I had not noticed them before, yet, instantly I knew what the glass fragments were.

"They are trauma, Daddy, aren't they?"

The Father smiled gently and nodded.

"Up until now, beloved, they were so deeply embedded in your soul, that they were not externally visible. But now, your mind is healing from the long season of sickness and trauma and they are being exposed."

I nodded. I knew that this was indeed the truth.

I looked back down into the box and slowly lifted away the second layer of tissue paper.

I gasped. There lay a pale blue dress in the exact shade of robin's egg blue that I loved so much.

I held it up and instantly I was wearing it.

It was so utterly beautiful.

"Thank you, Daddy! Thank you – it's beautiful!"

Then I looked down and saw there was a huge seeping bloodstain over my heart.

I looked up in horror at my Heavenly Father.

"It is the wound of abandonment," He said softly.

"When you were sick you experienced deep wounds of abandonment. You did not understand why such a thing could have happened to you. And so you felt unprotected."

The Father closed His eyes as though in great agony of soul.

"You thought I failed to protect you."

I stood silent before Him.

For I knew it was all true. Although my spirit always knew otherwise, my heart had been so intensely assailed by the enemy, that indeed I felt during the worst, most awful physical suffering that my Heavenly Father had abandoned me.

"But you understand more now."

"Yes," I whispered.

"My child, beloved child of My heart.

"I watched you. Crying for you. Yearning for you. Yet knowing that eventually you would return. In your most intense suffering, although you were not aware, I never left your side."

The Father picked up the most exquisitely cut glass canister filled to the brim with a liquid.

"These are *your* tears that you shed during your time of intense trial."

He picked up another much, *much* larger canister.

"And, these are the tears that I shed. For you."

And the Father lifted the canister of His tears and poured them over the blood seeping from my heart.

Instantly the blood stopped flowing and a great comfort washed over my heart.

"I will *never* abandon you. There is much, much more that I have yet to share with you, about the great sifting of the saints. But your heart is not yet ready."

He smiled tenderly at me.

"There is another present."

I looked into the box. There was more tissue paper. Slowly I lifted it up.

"Oh!"

This was the present of all presents.

It was a pen. It looked like a fountain pen.

I delicately picked it up and walked over and handed it to the Father.

I wanted Him to keep it for me.

"Watch." The Father picked it up, opened it and wrote.

Immediately blood and fire flowed from the pen.

"This is your pen, beloved.

"When you write, you will write by the shed blood of My Son and by the fire of My Holy Spirit. Without it, your words hold no power to change lives. With it, beloved child – a great impartation of My love – a great healing shall flow from the pages you write into the hearts and minds of those who read."

He laid it tenderly on His table.

"I shall keep it for you here. Never write without coming here first and picking up the pen from Me."

I looked longingly at Him.

"I will, Daddy. Daddy, you are so beautiful," I whispered.

"You are so beautiful, My beloved child."

And once again, like a little child, I jumped on the Father's lap and snuggled into His chest.

"Tell My children," the Father's voice was filled with tenderness, "Tell My sons and daughters how I yearn for them; how I long for their fellowship. That I will never, never abandon them."

I yawned. I was now tired.

"Of course, I will, Daddy."
And I fell asleep in my beautiful Father's everlasting arms.

MY STORY – SHAKEN TO THE CORE

*L*et me start at the beginning.

Beloved friend, if you're reading these words and have recently been or still find yourself in a place of intense testing and adversity, I believe that the Lord has asked me to share my story honestly, so that if you are facing severe adversity, momentary affliction, not only physical sickness, but bereavement, loss or heartbreak, loss of a marriage, loss of your business, your home, of so many dreams – you can know that there is such *real hope* for you ahead.

In April 2010, Rory and I had been stuck in New York during the Icelandic volcanic eruption on our way to Israel, and I had woken in the hotel with strange virus-like symptoms.

We arrived in Israel a few days later and although we had just been through one of the hardest financial challenges in the ministry of our lives, I had been in one of the best places I had ever been spiritually.

In fact, I remember spending time at the altar in our television studios in Jerusalem by myself feeling one of the strongest anointings of the Father that I had ever sensed.

That same week, I had actually seen the glory cloud *visibly* manifesting as a thick white smoke filling the studio at the close of one of our TV programs.

Yet, even though *I* had been steadfastly standing against the physical symptoms, worshipping, standing on the Word for healing, and in union with my Heavenly Father, as yet, I had received no physical breakthrough.

What I'm about to share is to impart a greater understanding of the incredible doors that were opening in our high call to impact the secular media mountain and the violent assignment that was released from the kingdom of darkness to stop us in our tracks.

Rory and I had carried a vision in our hearts to produce A-grade Hollywood films that would cross over into the secular, for over twenty years.

Our background, before we launched the UK and Europe's first Christian television network, GOD TV, had been in advertising and producing secular television commercials.

We had received numerous prophetic words about our apostolic breakthrough into Hollywood. Before I even met or knew our friend Shawn Bolz, he was literally stopped in his tracks by Jesus, while walking on the Hollywood Boulevard Walk of Fame. Jesus instructed him to go into a shop and buy me a touristy key ring with cameras and a Hollywood sign and send them to me with a note that our film and book project 'Chronicles of Brothers' would apostolically break through the gates of Hollywood.

Our dear friends Kim Clement and Cindy Jacobs had seen the apostolic call to film over our lives for years and even the prophet Bob Jones continually saw two areas of major mandate over our lives – Israel and Hollywood.

All that, to share that GOD TV is our first fruits, but our heart has always burned with the Father's passion to affect multiple millions of this generation who would never set foot inside a church through the end-time book and movie series 'Chronicles of Brothers.'

About a month earlier, the producers of the DVD edition to Warner Brothers TV series *Supernatural* had contacted me to film an interview on the first book in the series, *The Fall of Lucifer* (the Father's story), which I did, always excited about media evangelism.

A few weeks later, my London book agent had contacted us with the news that top ex-New Line film executive, who had been head of their European division for over eighteen years in London, had just read the first book in my series 'Chronicles of Brothers' – *The Fall of Lucifer*, had loved it and asked for a meeting.

So, on our return to London after our television stint in Israel, we met this producer for breakfast at Claridges.

It was a wonderful meeting, and we left agreeing that Ileen Maisel, the producer, would read the next two books in the Chronicles of Brothers series – *Messiah* and *Son of Perdition*, and if she loved them as much as the first book, we'd have a second meeting.

Things progressed rapidly from there and at the second meeting Ileen – (exec producer of *Golden Compass*) said how much she completely loved the books.

She was convinced that the world was desperate for this message and that the book series 'Chronicles of Brothers' *must* be turned into an A-grade secular blockbuster film.

She asked if she could send the books to her Los Angeles partner. We said, "Of course."

It turned out that her business partner was none other than Mark Ordesky, executive producer of *Lord of the Rings*.

Things progressed fast.

Two months later, initial contracts between our secular production entertainment company, Warboys Entertainment, and Mark and Ileen were signed in Los Angeles.

Just to add, we lived in Kansas at the time and God had given our dear friend Mike Bickle such a passion for Warboys and our vision to see the Chronicles developed into film.

Ileen was genuinely passionate about the subject matter of Chronicles. She visited us at our home in Kansas for a week for a mega story meeting for the Chronicles movie.

It was so exciting. The vision Rory and I had held in our hearts for over twenty years – to influence a billion souls through secular film, to apostolically take the entertainment mountain, had begun.

The devil feared this media call. And he was enraged.

How enraged, I was soon to discover.

Ileen and I spent days tearing apart my fourth draft of the screenplay of *Fall of Lucifer*, preparing it for the big screen, and that Sunday night Mark Ordesky flew from LA to us in Kansas and we all had dinner at Jack Stacks in Kansas City.

The vision for A-grade media projects to evangelize the unchurched in excellence for the Lord was on its way.

I was still not well, but continued to confess and stand on the Word, trusting the Lord for complete healing.

Mark Ordesky and I were already emailing back and forth different portfolios of prospective conceptual artists for the movie development process.

Mark and Ileen had handpicked others to receive my draft of the screenplay. They all loved it. The next step for me was to edit it down on a semi-final rewrite to a $150,000,000.00 budget.

I started my edit on the screenplay, little knowing that my entire world was about to fall apart.

One week later, precisely, I was hospitalized with the most intense nausea that not even the strongest anti-nausea drugs could stop.

Nothing could stop the intense physical suffering.

Tests. Tests. More tests. Then more tests. And more.

In between, our dear friends, Mike and Diane Bickle at IHOP, compassionately prayed for me. For which I am forever grateful.

More tests.

In between I prayed with wonderful intercessors in Kansas, to cut off all generational ties; we prayed every prayer imaginable.

Made sure I was walking in the light. In as much forgiveness as I knew how.

Then the specialists said triumphantly, "We've got the 'sucker'!"

I was so happy. So relieved.

Now I would be mended.

If only I had known.

The sucker was a rare condition known by the name gastroperesis.

They believed mine was viral. That a virus had damaged the vagus nerve, which led to a slowed-gut motility, which in turn caused intense nausea and almost total inability to eat.

I had such high hopes.

Now these horrific symptoms could be treated and I could go back to work in GOD TV, finish book four of the book series, Chronicles of Brothers – *A Pale Horse*, and continue with the movie development.

Unfortunately gastroperesis was rare and the medical knowledge of how to treat it was still mostly in an experimental stage.

The first drugs worked fairly well for me, but after three weeks I had to be taken off them because of the side-effects.

The second and third courses of drugs didn't work.

And there were no more options.

I was sick from morning till night.

Our Christmas that year, I spent weeping while my poor family tried to enjoy Christmas dinner. Even though I was standing on the Word, listening to Kenneth Hagin and every Word teacher I could get my hands on, my symptoms grew worse.

I couldn't eat. I dropped from a USA size six to a size two.

There was no respite. I fell asleep suffering. And I would wake shaking at 4:30 am to another day of intense physical suffering.

Finally, still in total faith that God had the answers, Rory and I flew to Philadelphia, to one of the very few gastroperesis clinics in the USA, believing I would find some key. Some answer.

By the time I saw the specialist, I was hardly able to eat, suffering from the constant debilitating nausea and had already dropped nearly twenty-five pounds in weight.

My heart was sinking from the questions he asked me.

Everything was still in experimental stages. I had had such faith to be healed.

I just didn't understand why I wasn't getting better.

And why there was no medical treatment that could alleviate the severity of the symptoms.

It appeared that there were only two treatments available that could possibly stop the extreme nausea and my inability to eat.

The first new medical option was to Botox my stomach.

The second option, which at that time was in the very experimental stages, was to implant a gastric pacemaker into my stomach.

The specialist immediately booked my stomach for the Botox procedure the following week.

Rory and I prayed about it and finally made a decision not to Botox my stomach.

To cut a very long two-year story short, through a number of divine circumstances, I arrived at a Christian naturopathic retreat in Germany.

I thought I would be there for three weeks. However, Rory, I, and our family were there for over six months.

I so deeply appreciated Wayne and Irene, who ran the retreat. The amazing thing was that Karina, the wonderful nurse there, understood gastroperesis – her own husband had suffered with it. No words can ever express my gratitude for all they did for me in that testing time – but for all of us, it was no easy fix.

For six months, I received infusions nearly every day. I was so used to tests and needles and blood draws – normally I'm pretty tough but because it was purely naturopathic I had to put up with extremely severe symptoms for a drawn-out period of time.

As anyone in the midst of chronic sickness will understand, to be continually sick every day and never to know when it will end – or indeed if it would ever end – except by faith is, I believe, one of the very toughest things one can face in life.

During that time the *Daily Mail* in the UK had a full-page article of a teenage girl who was diagnosed with exactly the same condition as myself and who had been on the verge of suicide because of the ongoing physical suffering. She was skin and bones.

Specialists in London had just implanted her with one of the very first gastric pacemakers and she was able to eat again. She felt that her life had literally been saved. But it was all still experimental.

I started to have anxiety attacks from the simple trauma of being constantly sick.

For the next year what our TV viewers had absolutely no idea about is that Rory and I and our family lived out of two suitcases in clinic rooms or motel rooms in Germany, Florida and Redding, California.

My children, who were bewildered and somewhat angry, found themselves in limbo, as did Rory.

Our dogs and cat were in kennels for an entire year.

Our home in Kansas was left abandoned for an entire year.

I couldn't function on a day-to-day basis.

I couldn't look after my family.

I couldn't manage my Production and Creative teams at GOD TV, let alone go on air.

I couldn't even *read* a book – let alone write one.

My ministry at GOD TV was over.

My writing ministry was over.

And the movie had obviously come to a grinding halt.

I didn't only 'feel' that I had lost my *life*.

Practically, I *had* lost my entire life.

Literally everything was not only on the altar: It was *gone*.

I was completely trapped in this debilitating chronic sickness.

Finally I reached the stage where I just couldn't face waking up to another day of physical suffering, another day of twenty-four-hour nausea. I was trapped.

I wanted it all to end.

ABANDONMENT

*T*he *truth* was that I felt totally abandoned by the God who had always been my all in all.

I just would have rather been in Heaven than had to cope with this unendurable physical suffering.

Now I knew why Satan had said to God in Job, "Skin for skin."

You see, there's a reason why Satan said, "But touch him skin for skin."

Beloved, if you are reading this and you are chronically ill, or you have a family member or friend whose physical body has been torn apart by suffering and they can't function normally or function at all, please understand that it also has a direct effect on their mind and soul.

It is a very different issue to go through an operation where there is a distinct goal and you know that after the operation your body will most likely be mended.

It may need time to heal, but you will be on the road to freedom.

What I'm addressing here is the Father's absolute mercy and compassion for those who feel locked physically in an unending cycle of physical suffering where they can see absolutely no way out.

There are only two eventualities.

To be healed or to stay trapped in chronic illness.

When Job was tested by the devil physically, the enemy's major strategy was to vex his spirit and to try to break his mind; to question God's faithfulness and His character.

There were two things that exacerbated the trauma for me.

One was that for the first nine months I took only the naturopathic route which did not alleviate the severity of any symptoms.

Secondly, was the immense pressure of some of those directly around me whose continual message, both subliminal and spoken, was if you don't have enough faith, you won't be healed.

You have to have faith.

Beloved suffering child of the Father – for many people locked in this kind of severe physical suffering their faith is *precisely* the enemy's target, made far worse by the fact that their human mind is reeling: "Father, why have You forsaken me?"

Reeling in abandonment.

To continually ask anyone who is going through the valley of the shadow where their faith is . . .

To inform anyone going through severe abandonment that if they do not have faith, they'll stay sick forever . . .

. . . Is today's form of a 'Job's comforter.'

For many who are chronically ill or facing the most intense trials, even the most *correct* Word of Faith theology, if it is *mixed with a religious spirit,* can easily become the 'Letter of the Law,' with the potential to weaken faith, rather than promote faith, because our focus becomes set on our **works**.

How much are we confessing the Word? Is our faith too small?

For many people, in situations facing severe physical sickness and severe adversity, their bodies and minds are already often stretched to their limit.

They are *fully aware* that they are fighting fear.

They are *fully aware* that their faith is on the line.

So when a well-meaning 'comforter' reminds them that 'what they fear will come upon them,' instead of building up their faith, it has the potential to fling them into further despair.

There is no one who knows the weaknesses of our own hearts better than ourselves.

The men and women who held out the greatest lifeline to me, as I walked through the valley of the shadow, were those who surrounded me with love. Those who consistently held my hands up when I was in my darkest place.

Who declared: "*We* believe. *We* are standing for you. *We will stand* in the gap of your weakness until you are delivered."

That is mercy indeed.

To bear one another's burdens in this situation is truly the love of Christ.

I know how hard it is to understand this until you have walked there.

The enemy's greatest assignment in tribulations and testing, apart from the hindrance of your God-given call, is to severely malign the very character of the Father.

Satan has lost his intimacy with our incredible Heavenly Father for *eternity*. Forever.

He is vehemently jealous of you and me as blood-bought saints – that now *we* have *access* to the secret and deep places of the Father's own heart.

And one of his greatest and most effective tools in this generation has been in both the secular world and in the Church to defame and malign the Father's own character.

He is the accuser of the brethren.

And a great part of that, in the searing heat of a severe battle, outworks itself in his accusations to our souls, to accuse our omniscient Father in our minds and hearts.

Satan tries to imprint his own character onto our Father's faultless, flawless one.

God has abandoned you?

Yet, Satan was the abandoner.

God is not faithful to you?

Yet, Satan is the eternally faithless one.

God's promises do not come to pass?

And yet Satan himself was called the father of lies by Jesus Himself. There is *no* truth in him.

And so day by day, the bombardments of the accuser, the maligner, accuse our faithful, unchanging, compassionate holy Father – of unfaithfulness, of treachery and of infidelity to us, His own children.

But, oh beloved, no matter the intensity of the furnace you may find yourself in,

Our beloved Heavenly Father *is goodness*

He *is faithfulness*

He *is the unchanging one*

He *is kindness*

He *is compassion*

He *is benevolence*

He *is joy*

He *is peace*

He *is love*

He *is grace – oh, so full of grace.*

Beloved one, if you're reading this today and you're walking through the valley of the shadow and loss, and experiencing severe feelings of abandonment –

Oh, let this start to set you on the road to freedom.

The Father is good.

The Father is the kindest One.

The Father is the compassionate One.

And He reaches out His hand to you.

And He would stroke your head and gently whisper to your heart, "Beloved, you *do* have faith.

"I'm not asking you to have faith in healing.

"I'm asking you to have faith in *Me*.

"I *am* Goodness.

"I *am* Faithfulness."

There were entire days when all I could scream out in my head was like the blind man, "Jesus, son of David, have mercy on me."

Do you realize that your cry of utter desperation to Jesus is faith?

Faith, in the one who you knew, if He was physically with you in your room, He would touch you and you would immediately be made whole.

When the body is tormented, you can reach a stage of such weakness.

The Father sees the huge reserve of courage, fortitude, endurance and perseverance just to survive another day.

But by the utter grace of God.

Through this darkest valley.

Instead of rejecting God.

Instead of denying Him.

I cried out *to* Him.

I did have some 'Job's comforters' around me, those who were full of formulas and the letter of the Law. But I also had Liz and Marilyn, my amazing old and trusted friends. And God gave me some incredible *new* friends during this time.

I will never, never forget how all these incredible friends and, many more that we cannot mention here, prayed for me.

They prayed for me, loved me and, most of all, never gave up praying.

And *never gave up hope*.

But the issue with a long and drawn-out sickness is that eventually everyone has to return to their own lives, no matter how much they love you.

I almost gave up hope.

While I was at the retreat in Germany, the Lord sent Ed and Ruth Silvoso to the area and by a series of miraculous events they visited us. Ed and Ruth had both experienced life-threatening illness in their walks. They were so understanding and so compassionate.

Ed shared that in his greatest hour of physical suffering, in agony of soul, that he cried out to God and asked Him to tell him if this was a sickness unto death or if he would live. He was in such anguish of body and soul, but he said to the Lord that if the Lord said to him that He wanted Ed to live, that he would take all his reserves even in the dark, dark place, and *fight*.

Ed also encouraged me to find medical, not just naturopathic help, at least to curb the intensity of the symptoms so that I could at least function in some capacity.

We finally went to Bethel Church in Redding, California, through Kris Valloton's kindness, to meet my now-beloved friend Julie Winter, a nurse practitioner who had helped Kris when he himself had been ill.

By the time I reached Redding, I had dropped to just over 105 pounds (around 7 stones), still barely able to eat or function.

And it was here at Bethel Church that I finally met Julie and her husband, Mike, who were so amazing and incredibly gracious, taking me into their home. It was under Julie's day-by-day compassionate care that I slowly continued to turn the corner.

Julie operates in the wisdom and discernment of God, and she started to find some medical answers.

I was still so sick that I was not in any way myself, but everyone at Bethel was so kind. Julie was on the board of Bethel Church, and Bill Johnson, who is just as wonderful as his books(!) would let me come in, sick and suffering, to the testimony meetings they have before the church services. The Bethel healing teams prayed for me so wonderfully many times.

I would love to tell you that everything was healed in an instant.

But the truth is that sometimes healing is a process; a somewhat lengthy process.

It took another eighteen months until I could finally eat normally and another year before I actually had months at a time free from nausea.

But the greatest scar was the trauma.

The trauma of why and how such a bad thing could have happened to me . . .

And how would I ever, ever feel completely safe again?

THE MEADOW

I had suddenly had an urgency to 'play' and felt quite guilty about it.

I had worked incessantly all my life, having grown up with a mother whose work ethic was extremely serious. The net result was that subconsciously, I felt guilty if I played.

Rory bought me a doll's house for my birthday, and I spent a good many hours dreaming about decorating it and on Etsy, an online marketplace!

And I had started using the creative social media site, Pinterest, and was 'pinning' each night for literally hours.

"Daddy, I'm pinning and buying stuff for my doll's house . . . I should be talking and visiting you . . . ."

"*Rest* and *play*," the Father said.

"*Rest* and *play* . . . ."

Then, while away in Israel, during a GOD TV Mission's week, the Father started taking me up in the spirit to a meadow.

These encounters lasted each night from midnight onwards, for a period of many months.

And with each encounter, I was gradually finding more freedom.

I would find myself by the spirit in a vast meadow filled with beautiful spring flowers.

Far to my left, I would see my wonderful earthly father in his heavenly garden.

He would often be standing at an easel, painting.

Then he would lift his head in ecstasy and cry, "To the GLORY OF GOD!"

Now, my Dad, who was a doctor, had died when he was 92 and had been blind for the last few years of his life. And now here in Heaven he was painting and was in his absolute element.

And, oh, how he had loved his garden – and his garden here was just beautiful!

To my right, also further off, was my Heavenly Father's rose garden.

So, I was continually in the middle of both my Heavenly and earthly fathers' gardens.

I seemed to be around the age of four.

I would be sitting on the ground in this amazing meadow of incredibly beautiful flowers, but directly around me was sand, so I was continually building sand castles.

Night after night I would find myself in this same meadow, singing like a toddler, happily playing, building sand castle palaces, blissfully unaware of anything else in my world.

Far, far below me was a huge battlefield where the great armies of the King warred.

But every time I was in the meadow, I was doing nothing else but playing.

Playing. Dreaming. Building sand castles. More playing.

Somehow I knew that my Heavenly Father was watching me intently from His rose garden.

Then, one day, in the first couple of weeks, I remember putting my hands to my head and feeling my blood seeping as huge, ugly, jagged pieces of glass fell out of my scalp, down onto the sand.

The pieces of glass hurt my fingers.

They were much, much larger than they had been a few months before on my birthday.

There was already a large pile of jagged glass next to me.

As more and more glass fell from my head, the more I played.

And the angels swept it up and gathered it.

Ministering angels, who seemed to wear mantles with red crosses, very quietly tended to my wounds.

Although most of the glass was coming out of my head, there were now also shards coming from my heart and there were great bruises on my arms and legs.

The angels, without a word, just continued quietly tending to the very raw wounds with vials of oil, tenderly, tenderly ministering to me.

And I, almost oblivious to all this, just carried on playing.

This continued for weeks, even several months.

Each night, as I closed my eyes, I would find myself back in the same meadow.

The more I played, the more glass fell from my head.

I knew that it was trauma being evicted from my body.

But I thought to be healed of the trauma I should be quoting the Word incessantly . . .

Not *playing* . . .

"*Rest . . . rest and play . . . .*" ·

This happened night after night.

Each night more jagged glass fell to the ground and the angels gently tended to my wounds.

But always to my right was the Father's own garden and the Father Himself would be walking, sometimes standing quietly, just watching me protectively as I played.

"Daddy."

I looked up towards my Heavenly Father in His garden.

"Daddy, what is happening?"

"Your wounds are the wounds of a great battle, beloved.

"The glass that falls from your head is trauma.

"The more you play, the more you rest as a little child in My presence, and the more healing of your body and your mind takes place on Earth.

"Every time shards of jagged glass fall from your head it means that the trauma is falling from your mind.

"Beloved, many in My Church do not yet understand how to heal those that have been wounded in battle.

"That is why it is so important that every wounded warrior runs directly to Me.

"For in this present Church age it is sometimes I, and I alone, who can bring the healing balm that is essential to heal the wounds of this present age."

"But, Father," I hesitated.

HARD QUESTIONS AND
HEAVENLY ANSWERS

"*D*addy . . . ."

I sighed. There were still so many questions I had concerning the past year's trials.

"You may ask . . . ," the Father said.

"But, Daddy, I thought I'm just supposed to let it go?" I muttered feebly.

If the truth be told, I had actually been going around and around and, thanks to my ever-inquiring brain and had nearly driven my friends and family to distraction wanting heavenly answers to 'why did this happen to me,' so it was fitting that finally I actually asked my Heavenly Father!

I almost felt Him sigh, not in exasperation, but with the kind of amused sigh a mother gives a much-beloved, stubborn and very persistent child.

"Beloved child – I formed you in your mother's womb. I designed your very inward parts – how much more did I design your mind?"

"I thought that I was just supposed to put the last season away," I mumbled, " . . . and not ask questions."

Now I felt the Father laughing.

"It's been almost *impossible* for you, hasn't it?"

"Yes, Daddy, it has," I said sheepishly.

I so wished that I could have been like many around me who could just put things like this aside, but I just could *not put it to rest.*

I hesitated.

"You mean You actually don't mind if I ask You?"

"My child, it is true that there are things that need to be left and no questions asked, but, beloved child of My heart, there are times that only if the questions are asked and truly answered that you can find the rest that enables you to let the past season go. *This* is such a time. Now ask your questions."

"Okay, Daddy."

There was a long silence. The Father waited for me to continue.

"Daddy, please – I really need to know why – how that happened to me," I blurted.

"You mean why something so bad happened to you – why you were sick?"

"Yes."

"And you have been bewildered and confused, because you were in intimate fellowship with Me when it happened?"

"Yes, Daddy, *You* know our verse . . . ."

My favorite verse in the whole of the Old Testament was from Psalm 91:

BECAUSE HE HAS SET HIS LOVE UPON ME, THEREFORE I WILL DELIVER HIM; I WILL SET HIM ON HIGH, BECAUSE HE KNOWS AND UNDERSTANDS MY NAME [HAS A PERSONAL KNOWLEDGE OF MY MERCY, LOVE, AND KINDNESS—TRUSTS AND RELIES ON ME, KNOWING I WILL NEVER FORSAKE HIM, NO, NEVER].

HE SHALL CALL UPON ME, AND I WILL ANSWER HIM; I WILL BE WITH HIM IN TROUBLE, I WILL DELIVER HIM AND HONOR HIM.

WITH LONG LIFE WILL I SATISFY HIM AND SHOW HIM MY SALVATION.
(Psalm 91:14–16)

That felt like my life verse. And yet it felt as though my whole life had been ripped apart and I was going through the valley of the shadow.

"Daddy, as far as I know, I wasn't in unforgiveness, I was checking my heart – trying to walk in as much light as I could. I wasn't perfect of course."

I grinned.

I felt the Father's humor. He well knew!

"And so you felt, My beloved child – that you were protected against serious attack."

"Yes, Daddy, I really did."

"And when you entered into a season of outright warfare and intense physical suffering, you could not understand how this could have happened? And it felt as though I was not there?"

"Daddy, I was so desperate."

I had walked through many, many battles prior to this, but none that was so intense when it came to physical suffering.

"It said You would protect me because I acknowledge Your name?

"I will call upon You and You will answer me.

"You will deliver me and honor me."

"Beloved – My beautiful, beloved child – remember, I said that there were things you were not ready to hear. I am about to share some of those things with you."

I waited.

"Because you greatly love Me – like many others reading these words, and have been chosen before your conception, like all my sons and daughters, to have intimate fellowship with Me – My enemies have become your enemies."

"Yes, Daddy, this I know and understand."

"Satan – cannot hurt *Me*. But he is vehemently jealous of those who now intimately fellowship with Me.

"He asked for permission to sift you, child.

"Even as he asked to sift Job and Peter and the disciples.

"Many of My children are at present going through a season of intense sifting.

"Let me tell you a story, a parable."

I snuggled deeper into the Father's lap and closed my eyes.

"This story is not just for you, beloved, it is for many of those who have suffered greatly in this past season.

"Who have entered the valley of the shadow of death.

"Oh, how much I love them and have yearned for them.

"Many of My children have believed that I have abandoned them.

"Listen to My words carefully, for they will deeply heal your heart. And heal theirs also."

I felt the Father stroke my hair.

"There was once a princess – a princess who grew up close to the King, her father. So close, that she was the apple of His eye – and He was her beloved Father. Her Daddy. Her protector.

"From the time she was just an infant, they fellowshipped together. They played and sang and danced and laughed together.

"How they loved each other.

"The great King had a fierce and unrelenting enemy. Before the princess was born, he had been second only to the King himself and had lived in the King's palace, in the throne room. But his pride and his jealously caused him to be banished from the Kingdom. And year by year, he turned crueler and more jealous of any that became the King's close companions.

"When the King created a new family – the King's enemy's wrath knew no bounds.

"But he was powerless against the great majesty and wisdom and goodness and power of the King and His Kingdom.

"The King stood up and gave a mighty decree. That all who served Him in spirit and in truth, and who set their love and allegiance only on Him would always be protected and know the King's protection.

"This caused the King's enemy to rise up in a great fury.

"As the princess grew, the enemy set his sights on her in particular. For, oh how she loved the King. To be with Him; to serve Him. Her whole life was solely intent on fulfilling His commands.

"But the King's enemy could not get near. Or even close to her. At every turn, she was protected by the King and His warriors.

"The princess grew into a young woman.

"She now ventured out beyond the palace and was always attended by the King's Royal Guard.

"The enemy launched many attacks against her on the highways and byways, but although there were some seemingly close calls, not one hair of her head was ever touched.

"And the enemy in great fury drew back to his macabre throne room in his fortress and schemed and schemed.

"Then finally he requested an audience with the King.

"The princess was greatly disturbed for her Father – the great King was deeply sorrowed. She had never seen Him so troubled.

"She ran up the aisle, and placed a garland of beautiful spring flowers upon His head and kissed Him on both cheeks.

"'Daddy, you are so beautiful.'"

"The great King looked upon her with such love – then took her in His arms.

"My child, how much do you love Me?"

The princess stood back in shock.

"Why, Daddy, you **know** how much I love You, with everything that is within me."

The great King looked upon her, loving her.

"My child – there is coming a season of testing. Much testing. Know this – I will never, never abandon you."

"Of course You'll never abandon me," the princess cried gaily. "You are my Father. I am your beloved. The beloved of Your heart."

And the princess ran off to continue her royal duties.

The great King put on his rubied crown and His mantle. He sat down on the throne and He lifted His scepter high.

"Let him enter," He cried.

The enemy of the great King walked in triumph down the aisle of the throne room.

"What is it your request?"

"I sue for Your favor."

"You know you do not have My favor."

"I have come from roaming throughout the Earth, going back and forth on it."

Then the Great King said to His enemy, "Consider My beloved princess. There is no one on Earth like her, she is blameless and upright, she fears God and shuns evil."

"Does the princess fear and love you, great King, for nothing?" the enemy replied. "Have you not put a hedge around her and everything she has?

"You have blessed the work of her hands. But now stretch out Your hand and strike everything she has, and she will surely curse You to Your face. Wherever she goes, she is surrounded by Your Royal Guard, or Your warriors. Every step of her life, You have surrounded her and protected her.

"But take that protection away and you will soon see her allegiance depart from You."

The Lord spoke to His enemy, "Very well, then; everything she has is in your power, but on My daughter – the princess – " He stood. Fierce. "But on her do not lay a finger."

"Ha – You know I still have the legal right of access. I sue for the princess."

"I will remove the Royal Guard for a season. But you will see you are wrong."

The King's enemy smiled maliciously.

"That is all I ask."

The next time the princess rode through the woods, she was set upon by the King's enemies. They stole her chest of rubies and gold. But because she had been trained for years, she and her one faithful courier put up such a fight that the enemy's guards went running back in shame.

The princess arrived home bruised and bloodied but victorious. She ran immediately to her Father, the great King, who held her to His chest.

And oh, how she loved Him.

The next day, the enemy of the great King returned.

He strode up the aisle where the great King sat on His throne.

The great King spoke quietly.

"Consider My beloved princess. There is no one on Earth like her.

"She is blameless and upright. And she still maintains her integrity, though you incited me against her to ruin her without any reason."

"Skin for skin!" Satan replied. "A man, a woman will give all he has for his own life. But now stretch out Your hand and strike her flesh and bones, and she will surely curse you to your face."

The great King was silent for many minutes. Then He raised His head to His enemy; tears were streaming down His face.

"Very well, then," His voice was barely audible. "She, My beautiful daughter, is in your hands."

The great King was moved with sorrow; he rose and departed from the throne room, turning once more. Fierce.

"But, you must spare her life."

THE GREAT SIFTING – THE WEARING DOWN OF THE SAINTS

*T*here was a long silence. I raised my face from the Father's chest.

"Daddy – You're talking about Job."

"Yes," said the Father.

"I'm talking about Job.

"And I'm talking about you and all who in this past season of intense testing on Earth have found themselves walking through the valley of the shadow.

"There are many at this moment who are facing trials that are direct warfare and easily discerned. There are others who are experiencing attack, through unhealed wounds and through areas of vulnerability, where the enemy has found access.

"But there is yet a third group in this hour.

"Those of My children, who have been sifted, not by My hand.

"But by the enemy's hand."

I snuggled further into my Father's chest.

I sensed a glimmer of a smile on the Father's face.

"You may as well say it," he said.

I lifted my head, still as a four-year-old.

"But I don't *believe* in sifting, Father!" I declared.

There was a very long silence. The truth was that I also didn't want to write about sifting, as I was well aware of the controversy it would cause.

"I mean – I grew up in the strongest time of the Word of Faith movement . . . ."

I was extremely thankful that the Father has such an amazing and forbearing sense of humor.

He totally ignored my theological standpoint and continued.

"Many have been sued for by Satan in this past season on Earth.

"Many of My dread champions, both known and unknown.

"Apostles. Prophets. Seers. Intercessors.

"Those called apostolically to take dominion of the mountains of kingdom government.

"All those that Satan and his principalities and powers recognized My mantle upon – the reason for the season of violent assault upon My Church.

"Satan himself is terrified. He fears these ones and the next great move of My Spirit greatly.

"He fears these, My servants, because Heaven is about to invade Earth. Because there is about to come the greatest move of My Spirit released upon the Earth that has ever been known.

"So Satan sued for many of those who are called to take up position in this outpouring.

"To launch such cruel attacks that their faith and trust will be totally shaken.

"Like a heat-seeking missile. Yes.

"The heat – the very fire of My call, My favor. My mark upon My sons and daughters in this season caught the enemy's full attention.

"Because of their call to dominion, their books were called up by the accuser of the brethren into the Highest Courts of Heaven – the High Courts of Justice. Thousands upon thousands of books from all across the Earth were brought by the accuser before the Chief Justices of the Councils of Heaven.

"Because of these ones' callings to affect entire nations and to bring kingdom government and dominion to apostolic areas of rule in the

Earth, these warriors have been anointed by My Holy Spirit to apostolically walk through the very gates of hell in the areas of kingdom government.

"To wrest the kingdom of darkness with violence and take it by force."

The Father was answering the question that had been burning in my soul for months.

In this past season, I had watched many of those that I knew to be totally sold out to the Lord, walking in the authority of the believer, who were strong in the Word and intimate with the Father be hit by such extreme and violent assaults on their families, ministries and bodies.

Some had lost sons, daughters . . . even babies.

Others had lost husbands and wives.

Many had been hit with cruel attacks against their bodies.

Still others had experienced tremendous financial hardship.

The unspoken question of my heart had been: *How – when we were walking as closely with the Lord as we could, when our greatest desire was to serve Him and to see His kingdom come?*

Yet, I and so many others had felt almost unprotected from the onslaught of the enemy in this past season.

There was a long silence.

"It is the unspoken question of many of My dread champions who have found themselves in the severest tests of their lives in this past season."

I waited. Silent.

"Eons ago, Satan himself was sifted.

"When he was sifted in these same High Courts of Justice, his heart fell to pride.

"He failed the sifting process.

"Now his demand in this past season, is as it was with Job — that My champions — those who professed to love Me more than their own lives, who had moved in greatest intimacy with Me. Those who had been given the mantle to demolish the kingdoms of darkness are sifted even as Job and Peter . . . and Satan himself."

"But Father . . . ."

I hesitated.

"That's not what I was *taught.*"

The Father waited patiently for me to continue

I had studied at Rhema College in the strongest time of the Word of Faith movement. "I was taught that the reason Job suffered was because what Job feared came upon him . . . ."

"But that is *not* what I said."

The Father's voice became sterner.

"My sons and daughters need to discern correctly the weights and balances placed upon certain aspects of My Word.

"They need to *rightly divide* My Word of truth.

"The words of Job were *not* My words.

"They were not even the words that My servant Job would have declared in his normal everyday life.

"These words were the desperate cry of a faithful servant of mine who was undergoing the most intense physical and mental anguish of sifting, pushed to the limit of his endurance.

"Not words on which to base an entire theology.

"Now study closely *My* words in this situation in Job 1 verse 8:

AND THE LORD SAID TO SATAN, HAVE YOU CONSIDERED MY SERVANT JOB, THAT THERE IS NONE LIKE HIM ON THE EARTH, A BLAMELESS AND UPRIGHT MAN, ONE WHO [REVERENTLY] FEARS GOD AND ABSTAINS FROM AND SHUNS EVIL [BECAUSE IT IS WRONG]?

"*Nowhere* did I say that Job was in fear or that he had opened his own soul up to be sifted.

"In fact, I said *very clearly* that there was none like My servant Job on Earth, that he was a blameless and upright man who reverently feared Me and shunned evil."

NOW THERE WAS A DAY WHEN THE SONS (THE ANGELS) OF GOD CAME TO PRESENT THEMSELVES BEFORE THE LORD, AND SATAN (THE ADVERSARY AND ACCUSER) ALSO CAME AMONG THEM.

AND THE LORD SAID TO SATAN, FROM WHERE DID YOU COME? THEN SATAN ANSWERED THE LORD, FROM GOING TO AND FRO ON THE EARTH AND FROM WALKING UP AND DOWN ON IT.

AND THE LORD SAID TO SATAN, HAVE YOU CONSIDERED MY SERVANT JOB, THAT THERE IS NONE LIKE HIM ON THE EARTH, A BLAMELESS AND UPRIGHT MAN, ONE WHO [REVERENTLY] FEARS GOD AND ABSTAINS FROM AND SHUNS EVIL [BECAUSE IT IS WRONG]?

THEN SATAN ANSWERED THE LORD, DOES JOB [REVERENTLY] FEAR GOD FOR NOTHING? . . .

BUT PUT FORTH YOUR HAND NOW AND TOUCH ALL THAT HE HAS, AND HE WILL CURSE YOU TO YOUR FACE.

AND THE LORD SAID TO SATAN (THE ADVERSARY AND THE ACCUSER), BEHOLD, ALL THAT HE HAS IS IN YOUR POWER, ONLY UPON THE MAN HIMSELF PUT NOT FORTH YOUR HAND. SO SATAN WENT FORTH FROM THE PRESENCE OF THE LORD.

(Job 1:6–9, 11–12)

"In the first chapter of Job, it was *Satan* who challenged Me and said that I had protected Job with My hedge of protection."

HAVE YOU NOT PUT A HEDGE ABOUT HIM AND HIS HOUSE AND ALL THAT HE HAS, ON EVERY SIDE? YOU HAVE CONFERRED PROSPERITY

AND HAPPINESS UPON HIM IN THE WORK OF HIS HANDS, AND HIS

POSSESSIONS HAVE INCREASED IN THE LAND.

(Job 1:10)

"It was *Satan* who said, 'take away your hand of protection and then see how Job will curse me to my face.'"

AND THE LORD SAID TO SATAN (THE ADVERSARY AND THE ACCUSER),

BEHOLD, ALL THAT HE HAS IS IN YOUR POWER . . .

(Job 1:12)

"Remember, Job passed the first assault of the enemy.

"Satan, knowing full well that he had failed, then tried his most cruel assault. He well knew that intense and unending physical suffering of a man or woman's physical body has the capacity to break a man or woman's mind and to vex their soul to the breaking point."

THEN SATAN ANSWERED THE LORD, SKIN FOR SKIN! YES, ALL THAT A

MAN HAS WILL HE GIVE FOR HIS LIFE.

BUT PUT FORTH YOUR HAND NOW, AND TOUCH HIS BONE AND HIS

FLESH, AND HE WILL CURSE AND RENOUNCE YOU TO YOUR FACE.

(Job 2:4–5)

"Not in one place in this conversation between Myself and the devil do you find *anywhere* where the reason for this sifting can be laid at Job's door.

"In fact, it was only when I *removed* the hedge of protection from My servant Job that the enemy was allowed to move in upon his possessions, his family, and finally to attack his physical body. Rightly divide the Word of truth, My child."

I sighed.

I still had more questions.

And the Father well knew it.

"I am answering your questions about the devil's ability to sift My saints today not only for you, beloved, but for many, many of My children who have been experiencing sifting in this present season, who have been bewildered because My Church has not rightly discerned My Word in this matter. Knowing what I say will set them free. Ask your next question."

I hesitated.

"Father, Job was sifted . . .

"And Peter was sifted, but surely after Jesus died on the cross and overcame Satan and the principalities and powers, surely Satan no longer has access to Heaven to accuse the Saints?"

"This is an important question, My child, and one that is essential for My sons and daughters to understand in these end times.

"Satan's first banishment occurred *before* Job.

"Yet he still had access to the Courts of Heaven.

"The major difference between Job and My children today is the *Atonement*.

"The issue is that My children may still be assaulted and violently sifted, but they now hold a major weapon against the devil in their arsenal: the Atonement.

"But even *after* the cross, the devil still has access to accuse the saints until he is thrown down to Earth by Michael during the Tribulation.

"In Revelation what do I say?"

THEN WAR BROKE OUT IN HEAVEN; MICHAEL AND HIS ANGELS WENT FORTH TO BATTLE WITH THE DRAGON, AND THE DRAGON AND HIS ANGELS FOUGHT.

BUT THEY WERE DEFEATED, AND THERE WAS NO ROOM FOUND FOR THEM IN HEAVEN ANY LONGER.

AND THE HUGE DRAGON WAS CAST DOWN AND OUT — THAT AGE-OLD SERPENT, WHO IS CALLED THE DEVIL AND SATAN, HE WHO IS THE SEDUCER (DECEIVER) OF ALL HUMANITY THE WORLD OVER; HE WAS FORCED OUT AND DOWN TO THE EARTH, AND HIS ANGELS WERE FLUNG OUT ALONG WITH HIM.

(Revelation 12:7–9)

"Now read the next verses."

THEN I HEARD A STRONG (LOUD) VOICE IN HEAVEN, SAYING, NOW IT HAS COME — THE SALVATION AND THE POWER AND THE KINGDOM (THE DOMINION, THE REIGN) OF OUR GOD, AND THE POWER (THE SOVEREIGNTY, THE AUTHORITY) OF HIS CHRIST (THE MESSIAH); FOR THE ACCUSER OF OUR BRETHREN, HE WHO KEEPS BRINGING BEFORE OUR GOD CHARGES AGAINST THEM DAY AND NIGHT, HAS BEEN CAST OUT!

AND THEY HAVE OVERCOME (CONQUERED) HIM BY MEANS OF THE BLOOD OF THE LAMB AND BY THE UTTERANCE OF THEIR TESTIMONY, FOR THEY DID NOT LOVE AND CLING TO LIFE EVEN WHEN FACED WITH DEATH [HOLDING THEIR LIVES CHEAP TILL THEY HAD TO DIE FOR THEIR WITNESSING].

THEREFORE BE GLAD (EXULT), O HEAVENS AND YOU THAT DWELL IN THEM! BUT WOE TO YOU, O EARTH AND SEA, FOR THE DEVIL HAS COME DOWN TO YOU IN FIERCE ANGER (FURY), BECAUSE HE KNOWS THAT HE HAS [ONLY] A SHORT TIME [LEFT]!

(Revelation 12:10–12)

"This takes place only during the Tribulation, child.

"As severe as things are presently on the Earth, Satan has not yet come to dwell on the Earth in fierce anger.

"This will not occur till the Tribulation.

"In verse 10, it is the accuser of the brethren who is bringing charges against My children day and night.

"Until the time of the end, beloved, until that day when Satan will be flung down to Earth by Michael, he still has access to accuse My children, and brings charges against them day and night.

"Always read in context, child.

"Now, remember My servant Paul and his thorn in the flesh?"

"Yes, Father. What has this to do with sifting?"

"Go back to My Word. The thorn in the flesh that was *allowed* because of the exceeding revelations he had received."

"Oh, no . . . ." I took a deep breath. *Now*, we were touching on even *more* controversial theology.

That also would not be accepted by some charismatic or Word of Faith theologians of today.

I could sense the Father smiling.

"I'm not scared of your *theology*, beloved. Paul's thorn in the flesh was a messenger of Satan."

I had read in a book written over one hundred years ago of a saint who had been to Heaven. The Lord had revealed to him that Paul's thorn was an actual man who rose up in great opposition to him.

"Yes, Father."

"My Son, Jesus, had already died on the cross when Paul was preaching.

"Is this true?"

I nodded.

"So the authority of the believer and the Atonement were already in place."

"Yes, Father . . . , " I answered hesitantly.

I knew exactly where the Father was headed.

Yet today in much of the Church, sifting by the enemy is discounted because of the cross."

"Paul's thorn . . . , " I whispered.

"But Father – certain ministers answer that by saying that *he* should have rebuked it, not to have asked You to rebuke it for him . . . ?"

I almost felt embarrassed repeating what was being taught in some circles of the Church.

"My servant Paul had one of the most profound revelations of the believers seated in heavenly places.

"My servant Paul was the very one who wrote about the authority of the believer. Do you not *think,* that if it had only been necessary to *rebuke it*, he would have done it? And what did I say?"

"You said, 'Your grace was sufficient . . . .'"

"Correct."

"Beloved child, what no one knows is that actually Paul's opponent was not there forever.

"But because of his great revelation he was sifted by the enemy.

"*That* is why My grace had to be sufficient for him for a season.

"This was AFTER the cross.

"If anyone had the knowledge and the power to rebuke the enemy in the revelation of the authority of the believer, it was Paul."

AND TO KEEP ME FROM BEING PUFFED UP AND TOO MUCH ELATED BY THE EXCEEDING GREATNESS (PREEMINENCE) OF THESE REVELATIONS, THERE WAS GIVEN ME A THORN (A SPLINTER) IN THE FLESH, A MESSENGER OF SATAN, TO RACK AND BUFFET AND HARASS ME, TO KEEP ME FROM BEING EXCESSIVELY EXALTED.

THREE TIMES I CALLED UPON THE LORD AND BESOUGHT [HIM] ABOUT THIS AND BEGGED THAT IT MIGHT DEPART FROM ME;

BUT HE SAID TO ME, MY GRACE (MY FAVOR AND LOVING-KINDNESS AND MERCY) IS ENOUGH FOR YOU [SUFFICIENT AGAINST ANY DANGER AND ENABLES YOU TO BEAR THE TROUBLE MANFULLY]; FOR MY STRENGTH AND POWER ARE MADE PERFECT (FULFILLED AND COMPLETED) AND SHOW THEMSELVES MOST EFFECTIVE IN [YOUR] WEAKNESS. THEREFORE, I WILL ALL THE MORE GLADLY GLORY IN MY WEAKNESSES AND INFIRMITIES, THAT THE STRENGTH AND POWER OF CHRIST (THE MESSIAH) MAY REST (YES, MAY PITCH A TENT OVER AND DWELL) UPON ME!

(2 Corininthians 12:7–9)

"Finally, remember Pastor Roland Buck."

My mind raced back to the late seventies when I had first been born again. Pastor Roland Buck had been an elderly, well-respected pastor in Idaho who had received many visitations from angels and had been taken up physically to the Father's throne room, where the Father Himself had given him a piece of paper listing several hundred separate events and people that he would meet.

Every single event on that piece of paper happened exactly as the Lord had said.

Even to the choosing of the Pope.

This was our sovereign God.

"Look to My Word, beloved. Many of My teachers here on Earth have been given a portion of My revelation. And it is tempting to look *only* at that portion.

"But know this, that the authority of the believer and My sovereignty over all those whose lives are fully committed to Me are *both* the spiritual truths of My Kingdom.

"They may appear to contradict each other.

"But they do *not*.

"They are equally important.

"And they need to be rightly divided and rightly balanced.

"Remember that true wisdom is not found in man's opinion; even the most spiritual man.

"It is found only in My Word.

"It is found only in Me.

"Now rest your mind, beloved.

"Come, it is time for me to show you the mantles My tested ones have earned as overcomers, through the sifting of their spirits, souls and flesh."

[YOU SHOULD] BE EXCEEDINGLY GLAD ON THIS ACCOUNT, THOUGH NOW FOR A LITTLE WHILE YOU MAY BE DISTRESSED BY TRIALS AND SUFFER TEMPTATIONS,

SO THAT [THE GENUINENESS] OF YOUR FAITH MAY BE TESTED, [YOUR FAITH] WHICH IS INFINITELY MORE PRECIOUS THAN THE PERISHABLE GOLD WHICH IS TESTED AND PURIFIED BY FIRE. [THIS PROVING OF YOUR FAITH IS INTENDED] TO REDOUND TO [YOUR] PRAISE AND GLORY AND HONOR WHEN JESUS CHRIST (THE MESSIAH, THE ANOINTED ONE) IS REVEALED.

WITHOUT HAVING SEEN HIM, YOU LOVE HIM; THOUGH YOU DO NOT [EVEN] NOW SEE HIM, YOU BELIEVE IN HIM AND EXULT AND THRILL WITH INEXPRESSIBLE AND GLORIOUS (TRIUMPHANT, HEAVENLY) JOY.

[AT THE SAME TIME] YOU RECEIVE THE RESULT (OUTCOME, CONSUMMATION) OF YOUR FAITH, THE SALVATION OF YOUR SOULS.

(1 Peter 1:6–9)

THE MANTLES

I raised my head and suddenly we were in what seemed to be a type of beautifully designed storehouse.

As far as my eyes could see, thousands upon thousands of mantles seemed to literally hover above the floor.

Some seemed to be fashioned of royal blue velvet.

Others of emerald, and I saw others of crimson velvet.

All with ermine fur at their collars.

Next to each mantle of this type hovered an enormous golden scepter with emeralds, rubies or sapphires embedded in the orb.

Then I turned and saw other mantles.

These seemed to be made of the most incredible gossamer-type fabric, literally shimmering with rainbow hues.

And next to each of these hovered intricately designed, silver scepters that seemed to radiate some form of blue electrical charges, like lightning.

Above each of these mantles was a delicate tiara, with one beautiful sapphire and aquamarine diamond in the very center.

Somehow, I knew that the velvet and ermine robes were governmental mantles for the apostles to the nations and apostles to the mountains.

The gossamer mantles were supernatural mantles of the Father's glory for the prophets and the seers and the watchmen.

I was about to move towards one that especially drew me, when I felt the Lord Jesus touch my shoulder.

"Beloved, before My children can put on their mantles, they must be healed of the trauma experienced from passing through long seasons of physical infirmity and the suffering they went through."

He looked at me with such intense love.

Intense mercy.

Intense compassion.

"You are greatly healed, but the long season of despair and abandonment has left you vulnerable."

Tenderly, He reached out His fingers and touched the fading scar that still encircled my head.

"In this next season, it is important that My dread champions who receive My mantles for the end-times battle that dawns.

"That any places that are still vulnerable to the enemy are sealed off by My Holy Spirit . . .

"The places of abandonment . . . the place of safety."

My heart sank.

For as hard as I tried, there was still in the deepest recess of my heart, a deep well of hidden fear that caused me to feel that I could never be completely safe again. That because my entire world, my very life, had been so ravaged *while* my love was set upon the Father.

How would I ever feel completely safe again?

It was almost as though I was living my entire life on guard.

That deep in my heart, no matter how my brain reasoned against it, my soul was still screaming; life is not safe even if you set your love upon Him.

Sometimes it was a memory.

Sometimes a triggered and intense fear.

I sensed the Father very near.

"Father, I have tried with all my strength, but my heart is still unable to rest in complete safety."

Instead of any condemnation,

Instead of any reproach,

I felt again such an intense love and compassion coming from the Father.

"It is not your job to try to once again feel safe, child.

"Relinquish your mind and heart to Me.

"Remember My servant Job."

I nodded.

"It was *my* hand of restitution.

"*My* hand of restoration.

"It was *My* right hand of *justice* that healed the final vulnerable places and scars from his mind and heart.

"Your final healing of trauma will not be dependent on YOUR works, child.

"It is now dependent on My grace.

"It is dependent on My goodness."

I knew the Father was smiling.

"Your only part in your healing, in this your final deliverance, is to rest in Me.

"For my goodness and My mercy shall surely find you.

"And shall follow you all the days of your life.

"And as it shall be with you . . . so it shall be with many others of My children."

The Father picked up an exquisite gossamer mantle that reflected light like a rainbow and held it over my head.

I started to panic.

"I am not ready, Father. You Yourself have said, I am not fully healed."

The Father gently placed the mantle over my head until it rested around my neck.

I felt the gossamer cloak billowing behind me.

The enormous weight of the mantle's glory was overwhelming. I could barely stand.

Then the Father placed the silver glowing tiara upon my head.

More heavy, heavy glory.

All at once it was as though my head was being anointed with oil.

There was a life verse on every mantle unique to the person it was created for.

Then slowly the Father handed me the scepter.

And the power of the supernatural authority surged like electricity through my fingers, right to my heart.

And yet, my heart still felt that awful unspoken dread of being unsafe.

"You still feel the effects of trauma."

I nodded.

"Even though you wear the mantle? Remember what I told you. This mantle is My great grace upon you.

"In not so many days, a new door opens before you and before many like you.

"A door of restitution.

"Of restoration.

"Of justice.

"I did not require you to be fully healed before you received your mantle.

"I only required you to understand that there are still vulnerable places that still *need* to be healed.

"In your weakness, even as My servant Paul, lies your strength.

"You see, My child . . . What is courage?" He asked me tenderly.

"Courage, Father, is when you're brave, and you don't fear."

"No," the Father smiled again with great tenderness.

"Courage, my beloved daughter, is not always the *absence* of fear.

"It is doing something even though you are afraid.

"*That* is what overcoming means.

"The greatest overcomers are those who overcome the most fear; the most traumas.

"Courage is often measured here in Heaven far differently than on the Earth.

"The times of greatest courage are often the times when My children are hit by terror and fear, and yet still they stand.

"Still they endure.

"Still they persevere.

"Remember, this one thing WILL remain."

"What is that, Daddy?"

"That all these ones hewn in the furnace of Satan's attacks and in the intense warfare of these end days.

"That these ones are Mine.

"They are MINE.

"They will have open access to My throne.

"They will sit on My lap and rest in My everlasting arms.

"They will whisper their deepest and innermost thoughts to Me.

"And I will whisper back to them.

"And they will hear My voice even as the voice of a mother, as the voice of a father.

"Even while they fulfill their destiny on Earth.

"These are the ones who will live often at My throne.

"Now, go, beloved."

Instantly I was surrounded by the Heavenly Host.

"You have been out of the battle too long."

The Father raised His hand.

And instantly I found myself in the Throne Room.

VOLUME TWO

THE END-TIMES CHURCH

*T*he Throne Room was almost indescribable in its magnificence.

It was so vast that it seemed to stretch all the way from the blazing white light of the throne itself to infinity.

It seemed that from where I was standing, there was no end to the chamber. And the focal point of the entire assembly was the huge throne that was shrouded in a living, shimmering white brilliance that illuminated the entire Throne Room.

Beyond the throne, millions and multiple millions, countless men and women of the vast unending assembly of the Sons and the Daughters of the Most High – those washed in the blood of the Lamb, were assembled.

And it seemed that, in that moment, I truly understood why in the New Jerusalem, the Scripture said that the glory of God would lighten the city and the Lamb would be the light of it.

For the Father's glory, emanating from the throne, illuminated the entire chamber with such a blazing holy brilliance, that I was almost blinded.

The Father of Lights.

AND THE CITY HAD NO NEED OF THE SUN, NEITHER OF THE MOON, TO SHINE IN IT: FOR THE GLORY OF GOD DID LIGHTEN IT, AND THE LAMB IS THE LIGHT THEREOF.
(Revelation 21:23 KJV)

And a great roaring sounded from the throne.
And thunder resonated from the throne.

And lightning bolts erupted that lit up the entire chamber and they seemed to carry the mighty, all-consuming glory of the 'Ancient of Days.'

Suddenly I was standing next to Jesus.

We were situated at the extreme right side of the chamber, just ahead of the Great Assembly.

Directly in front of us was the Throne of God.

And in front of the throne lay a book.

A book so enormous, that it lay almost as an altar before the throne.

I could not see the color of the leaves of the pages, because each leaf shone with such luminosity, that the book itself was barely visible.

And I sensed from the Angelic Host such a dread and a wonder.

The absolute *wonder* of what was in these pages.

I stood, utterly transfixed by the cascading waves of glory.

Waves and waves of literal, luminous white glory cascaded from the throne down upon the inhabitants of the Throne Room – until the entire assembly seemed to be bathed in the glimmering cocoon of soft white fire.

Then, suddenly, the Throne Room disappeared from view and I was standing with Jesus, looking down on a vast field before us that seemed to stretch for miles ahead.

"We will return to witness the opening of the Book . . . ," Jesus said softly. "But, My child, there are things we need you to see concerning the end-time church that you must share with others."

THE GARDEN

The field was completely bare, except for a thin, freezing blanket of white frost.

Above the ground, all over this freezing blanket, were thousands of tightly furled flowers that seemed to me to look like the crocus buds we know on Earth.

But these flowers were not in bud.

And there was no sign of life.

As I watched, a warm wind started to blow.

The sun rose high above the field and suddenly, from all four corners of the vast expanse, thousands of the most incredibly beautiful flowers began to blossom at a rapid rate, as though in some kind of intensely lit hothouse.

The flowers and the plants were *beautiful beyond description.*

I felt a prompting that they were 'in the image or imprint of their gardener.'

I distinctly remember seeing the most amazingly beautiful lilac and pink hyacinths. They were over six feet tall, and there were lilies – tall and splendid – pure and brilliant.

And then the Lord showed me some strange-looking plants that seemed more cactus-like in their appearance.

These were not at all as beautiful as the flowers seemed, and yet the Lord Jesus gazed at them with great tenderness.

And I knew that they were of exceeding worth to Him.

That they were the lives and ministries that had been birthed in the hard places: where no man has tended them.

They have so often been passed over and overlooked in place of those who to the outward eye were more seemly.

Yet, even as I watched – I somehow knew that these were the lives and ministries that the Lord Himself had intimately tended.

Slowly, Jesus reached down.

I watched as He cut the stem of one such plant and immediately great gushing waters poured out.

And it was as though I understood that those who had stood through the arid times, when there was little encouragement, when they were bare and dry, as they had sought their praise and approval solely from Jesus and the Father, so in turn now, because of their faithfulness they were to be containers and the 'out pourers' of His Presence – of revival fire – of unending floods of living water in this end-time battle that would literally water families, towns, cities and communities, ministering to the dry and thirsty with rivers of life from the source of living water that would never be quenched.

Then my attention was drawn to a far, far corner of the garden, where I saw bunches of smaller, wild-looking, brightly colored flowers that appeared to be growing crazily, almost unstoppable, with no pattern or order. And a great joyous, piping melody came up from them.

I watched as the Lord Jesus bent over and plucked the flowers.

There was such a look of joy and tender love on His face, and somehow I knew that He deeply enjoyed the hearts of these ministries who, in the face of all opposition and persecution, had overcome and were overcoming the fear of man enough to follow His voice and His Spirit above all others.

These were the ministries who seemed out of step to the church of the present day because they danced to a new sound from Heaven and piped a new melody to the Bride of Christ.

And although they were not yet fully understood by the five-fold ministry of the day, I knew from the Lord that this would change in the next coming season. For, they were intimately known and deeply loved and embraced by the Master.

Jesus placed them gently back onto the emerald-green grass and watched in joy as they continued to pipe and dance ahead of the field.

Now, amongst the beauty that was now arising all over the vast expanse, I saw two large trees that had grown seemingly out of nowhere and towered over the garden.

In fact, now that I looked, these trees were appearing on the surrounding edge of the garden.

These, I sensed, represented apostolic works in the Earth today – that had already provided much sustenance for the Lord's people and He was well pleased.

But I saw that in this next season there was to be a different mandate and an even wider influence because they had proven trustworthy in the past season.

As I looked at the trees in front of me, I saw huge branches start to grow from the trunks and roots go down hundreds of feet below the surface and suddenly many eagles, previously unseen, stirred as one.

Magnificent white and golden eagles flew from the branches.

I felt that because of the strength and sturdiness and expanse of their reach, the trees were apostolic, representing the structure developers and the builders.

The eagles, these were the Prophets and the Seers.

These were the Apostolic and Prophetic works that were rising in the Earth.

And I saw hundreds of animals and other wildlife able to take cover and find shade and protection from the heat and the wind and rain.

These ministries were definitely a place of refuge – a place of healing – a place of teaching. And even as the prophets worked and moved seamlessly with the apostles, in turn the branches were a place of habitation and safety for the prophets, I sensed.

And then a tremendous *fragrance* overtook the field. And suddenly, it seemed as though every perfume from each individual flower and plant and tree had been released as one glorious aroma that rose up to the Heavenly Father.

And I knew that it was received at the Throne Room with *uproarious delight* – a truly acceptable offering unto the Lord God of Hosts.

But then as I looked across the field – I realized that at the farthest end of the field – was a second field.

A lower field.

The lower field was a wilderness. Nothing grew. To the outward eye everything seemed dead.

And here the mud was caked and the ground was so bare and dry that nothing grew and nothing stirred.

There were many trunks of trees, but many of their limbs were broken off, lying on the ground.

They seemed to the outward eye to be completely dead.

And I sensed that the Lord was saying,

"These are those who have served Me for a long season, those who are right at this moment in a season of wilderness and drought and what seems to be in some areas of their lives, an area of almost death to everything.

"For many, this has seemed frightening and at times almost bewildering, for many of these have served Me fully, with an unwavering heart and devotion."

Next to this part of the garden, on the far, far side was an old and rusted gate.

It was very large and seemed as though it had not been opened for many, many years.

But now, beloved, there came a movement and suddenly that most glorious of footsteps came nearer. And as the Lord Jesus drew closer to the gate, the oil and Balm of Gilead flowed down from His anointed head, running over His hands, down His robe and over His feet and sandals as He walked.

And, as He neared the gate, He lifted His hand and turned the great iron clasp and as the oil literally dripped onto the clasp, with one easy, sliding movement, it opened.

And gently, so, gently, He walked. Single in His purpose.

He walked first to one bare trunk, and then another until each one had felt His presence.

And at each footstep, so beneath His feet immediately shoots of tender, new grass sprung up amidst a myriad of buttercups and spring flowers.

And as He placed His hands on the bare, seemingly dead trees the branches instantly grew with green buds springing from the bark.

And in almost what seemed an instant, the entire lower bare field was transformed into an orchard of the most exquisite cherry blossom trees I have ever seen and I felt that the Lord Jesus say,

"Visitation My child – visitation –"

"There is coming the day upon the Earth very soon, My child – when all those who have sought Me – who have yearned for My presence – who have stood strong even in the midst of death and destruction and of hurt and

of anguish – and of promises and visions not yet fulfilled – to these ones, beloved – comes My day of visitation – when I, Jesus Myself, shall be with My people.

"When they shall know the Balm of Gilead to heal their broken hearts – when they shall feel the oil of My presence and anointing wash over their souls – when they shall feel My healing touch even as it was upon the Earth when I laid My hands on the sick to make them whole."

And then, as I turned once more to look at the cherry trees, I saw suddenly that upon each now hung a large sign and, as I looked, I read 'HOPE' on one sign.

Another sign read, 'HEALING.'

Behind, in the next row, the sign read, 'FAMILY SALVATION'; another read, 'LAST DAYS MINISTRY.'

Another read, 'BROKEN HEART MENDED.'

Yet, another sign that I remember, read, 'BELOVED OF GOD.'

And I knew that from this particular visitation of the Lord Jesus to all in this lower field, many, many who had been called to this last end-time battle, who the enemy had tried to cut asunder by loss of hope, by sickness, by rejection, by hope deferred in their ministry vision. The loss of family loved ones by divorce or death.

Through this Visitation **whole battalions were being reborn**, strong in the hope and joy of the Lord Jesus Himself.

Healings manifested.

Children and families were saved.

Ministries were born.

Visions were newly established.

This same army that a few minutes before had seemed desolate and hopeless was now an army that was strong and fervent and full of the Word and the Spirit of God Himself.

Oh – how tenderly He loves you.

Oh – how much your love and your worship and your adoration in the unseen secret place has meant to Him

Oh – how greatly He has seen the work of your hands – the labors of your ministry as unto Him – although many may not have realized the cost in the midnight hour – the sacrifices of you and your family – your great love and your labor for the gospel have never gone unseen by Him.

He is the King of every king ever born.

He is the lover of your soul.

He is the Lord Jesus Christ . . . and He loves *you*.

Then the Lord lifted my head and I saw a concentration-camp-like structure before us that was some way away from the main garden.

And as the Lord Jesus gazed upon it, a terrible grieving passed over His countenance.

"My end-time church . . . ," He whispered. "Many who should be on the frontlines of the end-time battle are incarcerated in this, the enemy's camp."

"You mean the unbelievers?" I asked.

"No," the Lord whispered. "They are My children. Some have walked with Me intimately in previous seasons. They have become prisoners of war."

And immediately I saw two black signs with white letters drawn on them and the first read:

'P.O.W. – PRISONERS OF WAR.'

And then the second sign read:

'M.I.A. – Missing In Action.'

I followed Jesus as He walked towards the perimeter of the huge barbed-wire fence.

PRISONERS OF WAR

As I looked further, I saw thousands of men and women who seemed to be prisoners, walking or shuffling around the perimeter of huge barbed-wire fences.

Their prison uniforms resembled those of a Second World War concentration camp, but their uniforms were not all the same.

The prisoners on the left side of the camp had both their hands and feet shackled by heavy chains. In fact, the iron chains weighed them down to such an extent that they shuffled rather than walked. Many of these prisoners were stooped and bowed, almost doubled over.

As they shuffled and limped along in an unending, aimless single file past the perimeter, I could see signs on their backs but could not read them clearly.

This entire sector seemed to be dominated by one particular legion of demon keepers, who were taking untold relish in whipping them mercilessly as they continued their unrelenting path around the perimeter of the camp.

But it was the prisoners' faces and bodies that caught my attention.

Their faces were horribly contorted and twisted. And in their eyes was a terrible rage and fury that they should even be there as prisoners. Their limbs were, without any exceptions, completely twisted and knotted; their hands were misshapen and crippled.

Then I saw hunchbacks, many, many hunchbacks.

As I studied them more intently, I suddenly realized that the misshapen hunches had not actually been intended as part of their bodies and I now could read the signs on their backs – BITTERNESS,

WRATH, UNFORGIVENESS, SEDITIONS, CLAMORING and SLANDER.

I turned back hurriedly to look for Jesus in the garden, but He was no longer there.

Then I noticed an old man with white hair, simply dressed in a brown, homespun robe, with no great attractiveness of features, who stood quietly next to me, watching my growing consternation over the prisoners before me.

"They were once followers of the Lamb," he said softly.

I looked back towards the garden where the magnificent, beautiful flowers and plants were flourishing and shook my head vehemently from side to side.

The prisoners there before me bore absolutely no resemblance in any manner to anything or anyone who had enrolled in our amazing Warrior King's army.

The old man smiled gently, sorrowfully at me, as though smiling at a child who was dull of understanding.

"Come," he said, taking my arm and leading me closer to the perimeter of the fence.

As we approached, the prisoners at the edge of the fence pressed their faces to the barbed wire and grimaced, spittle running down their gnarled chins, jeering and clamoring.

Their ringleader was the most vocal and ugly of all – with a double hunchback. He held an iron cudgel in his hand and slammed it across the wire in rage, as near to myself and the old man's face as he could.

Slowly, the old man eased his right hand through the barbed wire and placed it gently upon the ringleader's knotted, hunched back.

I waited with bated breath, as all at once a soft, warm, fierce coral-colored wind blew across the entire camp, and the ringleader stared, as though one entranced, into the old man's eyes.

In an instant, I saw the ringleader's features change and soften, tears flowing unheeded down his cheeks.

And as I turned to look at the old man beside me, I wanted to fling myself to the ground as though one dead,

For, facing me was the Lord Jesus Christ.

In all His majesty.

In all His glory.

Over six foot tall, arrayed in the robes of the King above all kings.

His robes shone and flashed like lightning and they were silver and gold, but, as He turned, in an instant, they were aquamarine, emerald and deep royal-purple hues.

His skin was as burnished bronze.

His eyes were clear and fierce, yet they carried the mercy and the tenderness of all the ages.

He wore a sword belt around His waist that glistened with jewels of many hues.

And just before I, in turn, flung myself to the floor, I looked around.

Every prisoner at all four corners of the concentration-camp quadrant had fallen prostrate onto the ground, face downward, worshipping.

And then Jesus smiled – and the whole of Heaven was in that smile.

Gently, oh so gently, He took my hand, His right hand still on the ringleader's back and eased me back onto my feet.

"This man before you was one of My finest servants. He was a missionary in one of the most uncared for and un-evangelized parts of the Earth.

"It cost him greatly to leave his country and his home to do this work.

"He sacrificed greatly for me."

The ringleader now clung onto the Lord's hand desperately, as though never wanting to let it go.

"He served Me faithfully for many, many years, unseen by others, his family going through many trials of faith for My kingdom, fighting persecution, disease, deprivation. Even his church that had sent him didn't appreciate the magnitude of his and his family's service and sacrifice for Us.

"But he and his family were not unseen by Me and My Father, and his sacrifice counted greatly to Us in the courts of Heaven."

Now, the ringleader was sobbing, clutching at the Lord's robe through the wire.

Gut-wrenching, agonized sobs.

Then the Lord passed straight through the fence and held him to Him tightly, as a mother with a child and gently laid his head at His breast.

He looked at me with a terrible grief.

"After many years of faithful sacrifice, many new and younger missionaries came into his area and reaped greatly from the multitude of seeds he had sown in the hard and fallow ground.

"The area became such a harvest for souls that soon there were great accolades from all over the world for the new missionaries. They were invited to world conventions, received vast amounts of finance for their mission work and were lauded by the princes, kings and ambassadors of that region."

"And this man was overlooked," I whispered.

Jesus nodded. His eyes tender.

"Yes. No one, not even the new missionaries, gave him honor for the faithful tilling of the soil for years. It was not with intent. My young zealots were enthusiastic and still growing in My ways, but after all the hardship he had endured, it was too much for him to bear."

"But why is he *here*?" I looked in shock around me. "This is the *enemy's* camp, but look how he clings to you."

Jesus closed His eyes for a brief moment.

"He is a prisoner of war.

"He has been taken captive by the enemy.

"In his agony of soul at being overlooked and in his isolation, he quickly started to lose sight of the courts of Heaven and eternity and fell into a deep, deep depression.

"I sent some of My servants to deliver him and to lift him out of it, but he quickly came to the place where in bitterness of soul, he refused all offers of help.

"Then, because of that same bitterness, the demons started to torment him day and night, telling him that I had abandoned him."

I sensed this was very difficult for Jesus.

"Oh, beloved child of God, if only we could each realize the incredible magnitude of His love." Jesus' voice was very soft.

"Many of My children, in this end-time season have been experiencing abandonment through long, grueling seasons of persecution, sickness, or just a wilderness of soul.

"I said I will never leave you nor forsake you, that I am with you forever, world without end . . . . " Jesus wiped a tear from His eye.

"This was a man of great prayer and of worship. But, he stopped communing with Me and My Father. And the demons' voices held more sway in his mind and he started to heed them, becoming so filled with bitterness and unforgiveness that even his own family didn't recognize him.

"He left them and led by his demon captors, lived as a recluse, consumed by self-pity and bitterness, hating the Church and rejecting My people . . . and Me."

I looked in amazement at the ringleader on his knees, still clinging to the Lord Jesus' hands, his gnarled face bathing in the radiance from that most beautiful face.

"My Church gave up on him, until no one visited him, no one cared for him and he was left only with his torment."

Jesus was now weeping. It was very hard for me to bear.

To see the King of kings so grieved at the torment of one of His children.

His voice became very soft.

"If My children had kept praying for him, if they had kept blessing him.

"If they had loved him with a love that believes the best, that endures all things, that never fails, he would not be here today.

"In the evil that overwhelms the Earth today, it is imperative that My people bring the captives to Me in prayer. For it is their prayers that enable the visitation of My presence and My power to invade these captive lives.

"Tell My children to pray without ceasing for these ones, and to never give up.

"No, never give up.

"But *today*, someone has petitioned Me and My Father with powerful prayers for his soul . . . ."

Jesus looked at me.

"*This* is why I have been able to visit him today, here with you, My child . . . because someone travailed for him.

"My power alone is strong enough to liberate him."

The Lord placed both hands on the ringleader's back and immediately the two double hunchbacks were loosed and came away in Jesus' hands. And as they did, I saw inside them were great black worms and thousands of translucent eggs hatching. They all had names.

I saw some of them were VENGEANCE, FEAR, UNFORGIVENESS, HATRED, DISSENSIONS, DEPRESSION, SELF-PITY.

And, as Jesus lifted them off his back, the crippled, deformed limbs of the old missionary instantaneously became straight and strong.

The misshapen face became smooth and at peace.

The old missionary started to worship Jesus, literally, glory flooding from his face.

Questions flooded into my mind: *Who would look after him? What if we, the Church, didn't? What would happen to him?*

But the Lord drew me away from the scene and was walking to the far corner of the concentration camp where there was a completely different scenario.

Why, it didn't even seem like a prison, more like a holiday camp.

The prisoners wore bright, vibrantly colored, striped uniforms, with hats of all kinds and colors.

Bright vermillion-feathered hats, golf caps, Stetsons, beautiful black velvet, wide-brimmed hats, boas and masks of every description.

There was great festivity and everyone was continually feasting and drinking and partying to loud, incessant music. In fact, the music never stopped.

There were men with men and women with women and men and women together.

Everyone looked young and toned – it looked like a 'who's who' collection of 'beautiful people' – a far cry from the gnarled ghouls at the other side of the camp.

But as I looked nearer, their skin and eyes took on a glassy sheen, and I saw that they were zombie-like in their carousing.

There were gargantuan demon guards whipping them at intervals, and each time a whip came down, I saw LUST OF THE EYES, DECEITFULNESS OF RICHES, PRIDE OF LIFE . . . and a great sign rose over the gate reading – M.I.A. – MISSING IN ACTION . . .

MISSING IN ACTION . . .

I stood quietly right at the very edge of the barbed-wire fence, and somehow I knew that to draw attention to myself would not be wise.

I felt a warning from the Holy Spirit that even as so many, many years before I had found the Lord in the midst of a similar environment, that to expose myself to such a brazen array of these spirits, I could even now, put myself in grave danger. So I stood watching, silently.

I turned to find another onlooker, a girl who appeared to be in her twenties.

She moved from the fence and walked tentatively through the gate which was unlocked.

People could enter but once inside the gate, they had no need of a lock, as no one ever wanted to leave.

The girl walked into the prison and headed straight towards a very beautiful girl and attempted to pull her away from the partying.

I saw a group of snakes nestled in the captive girl's hat, poised to strike and, as the young girl tried to pull her friend away, an evil smile appeared on the young woman's face, as the snakes rose up, striking her rescuer with their fangs.

I saw two fangs bite deep into her neck and the poison seep into her body.

I started to run to help her, but just as I was about to leave the safety of the fence, I felt a gentle touch on my shoulder.

"No," spoke Jesus.

"The intensity of the spirits of lasciviousness and lust that have been unleashed against My Church today are very powerful.

"You may only go in there at the direction of My Father.

"Some of our greatest servants were struck by the serpents of lust.

"The lust of the eyes and the lust of the flesh and brought down to their knees, never to rise again in the glory ordained for them by My Father.

"This is a cunning, powerful spirit that is laced with enticements and all manner of demonic attachments to beguile and then finally enslave.

"You were rescued from that pit when you were very young.

"You cannot go back, except with Me and at My command."

I looked at the Lord questioningly.

"Then why am I here, Lord?"

He sighed.

"Today I have come to rescue one who is greatly beloved by Me and by My Father.

"One who suffers great agony.

"One, from whom the devil has tried to steal his very soul.

"I want you to understand how this came to be and to warn others."

Jesus pointed to one of the focal figures in the midst of the party.

He wore a bright vermillion hat and was virtually naked, his body painted in an assortment of bold colors.

Serpents were twisted around his lower body, and one was flung around his neck.

He drank from a great golden cup and caroused with vigor, committing multiple lascivious acts with fervency and with ease.

I saw nymph-like, male demonic forms caressing him and all the while ecstasy was rising in his eyes.

The rest of the lewd sexual acts he committed within that small party, both with men and with women, will not be mentioned here.

It was evident that this man was brazen in his sin and he definitely did not seem to want help in any measure.

I turned to the Lord, confused.

"He is Mine," the Lord said firmly.

"But Lord, You said to cut out your eye if need be? This man is enjoying every lustful pleasure. It is painfully obvious he does not *want* to be set free."

A great sadness crossed the Lord's countenance and He drew me nearer.

"What you see before you is his present state in the spirit realm.

"*This* is who he is and where he sits today."

The Lord moved His hand and I looked in on what I knew was a very, very significant meeting between government officials in Washington and the leading Christian voices in America.

They were discussing abortion and same-sex marriage and many issues of great importance to the Christians of America and beyond.

I frowned.

"I don't see him, Lord," I said, studying the faces of many leading ministers who sat around the table.

"He is there," the Lord said softly, pointing to one of the more well-known faces. One I knew to be a family man and a well-respected propagator of family values, decency and sanctity in marriage.

"No!" I said.

"It is he." The Lord looked at me with compassion.

"And I have come to rescue him today."

The scene changed and I saw the man in a hotel room, his clothes were off and he was engaged in lewd acts with a male prostitute.

The Lord bowed His head.

The scene instantly changed. And now I saw this same man, locked in his den, his all-American family playing, reading and praying throughout the house.

He was on his knees, wringing his hands, tears and mucus streaming down his face, banging his head against the floor, silently crying out, "Jesus, help me . . . Jesus, help me . . . Have mercy on my soul."

The compassion and the grieving of the Lord surged through me and tears rolled down my cheeks too, for I knew this man's works and I knew that he had for years and years truly loved and served the Lord.

"But how, Lord, . . . why?"

The Lord did not answer me, but took me to another scene; a scene far, far back in the man's childhood where I saw him as a young boy being bullied and then sexually abused by more than one.

"He came to the altar when he was young, for We had laid Our hand upon him. Our call upon him was great and he was to be raised up as a clear and clarion call to this generation.

"He married, went to Bible college, started a church and for many years he was able to fight the demons that sometimes assailed him.

"But as he rose up the ranks of My servants, the assignments became more intense and more frequent.

"He could have asked for help at any time.

"I placed around him many friends. True friends who would not have condemned him, friends who would have counseled him and given him vital tools that would have kept him free.

"He was ashamed of his struggles, but still, in his early years, he would confide at times to one he trusted."

The Lord was still for a moment and I could see the next sentence greatly grieved Him.

"But over time, as his voice became more influential, he became ambitious.

"And *his ambition caused him to greatly fear his sin*. And where, even in a moment at the start, he could have found deliverance if he truly sought it, he now shied away from any accountability, save for the very superficial areas of his life."

"For he did not want to risk losing his position . . . ," I murmured. The Lord nodded.

"He knew what he could become, he hated it, but he wanted his influence to continue.

"He knew the only thing that could impede his fast track to influence and leadership in the nation was the truth that lay behind the mask.

"He knew that if he was accountable, he would in most probability be counseled to take lesser visibility in public, Christian and secular arenas. *But he was not prepared to lose his position.*"

I watched as he traveled around America, preaching on family values, gaining influence, courted by both the Christian and secular media and I saw the assignment of the enemy accelerate.

I watched as demonic serpents were unleashed against him and the lascivious spirits would torment him at night with their enticements of the flesh and soon his dreams were filled with fantasies that his wife could never fulfill.

And I saw a black tentacle enter his mind, then it gave birth to more tentacles and these dropped into his heart. And, as the torment of the fantasies became more intense, he became obsessed with fulfilling the same fantasies.

And all the while, he preached to his church, prayed for the youth and influenced the influential.

Then the devil sent along his tempters to entice him, willing men who were ensnared themselves, men who did not know Jesus.

Men easily bought.

He paid for their favors.

And the lies became entrenched.

But still he preached and still he headed up gatherings in the name of Christ.

And once again, I saw him, pleading with God, hating what he had become, trapped in his own pretense.

Night after night after night, he would scream and cry out to the Lord to take him home.

"He has fallen so far, My child, that he cannot be saved without My direct help. But the pain he will endure will seem at first far, far worse than the torment he is enduring now.

"Wherever there is a life in strong deception, with truth comes exposure.

"I am the Truth.

"He has called on Me as truth and, as truth, I will come and deliver him.

"My Church is not without compassion, but he will face many judgments of his own making, for his sin was not just caused by shame but by pride.

"He will be deserted and scorned by many.

"He will be abandoned and despised by more.

"Many of those who trusted him most will be the most wounded.

"He will soon learn that the wages of sin is death to those he loves the most. And is death to all he knew and loved.

"The loss he would have experienced if he had asked for help when he knew he should is insignificant compared to the heart-rending loss he will experience now."

I followed the Lord closer towards the partying.

But the Lord waved me back.

"It greatly pains Me."

Suddenly the Lord's robes started to shine with a great white brilliance.

He walked nearer to the virtually naked form wearing the vermillion hat.

As He drew nearer, the demons screamed in high-pitched terror and fled.

Jesus grasped the main serpent around the man's neck and with His great strength ripped the snake in two and threw it on the floor.

I saw a sign over the snake that read DECEIT.

I then saw an angelic sign that read TRUTH, and I knew that for this man his deliverance would come through exposure.

Jesus grabbed the other serpents that were twisted around his lower body, LASCIVIOUSNESS, LUST and then I saw a Golden Dragon perched on his temple called PRIDE.

The Lord Jesus crushed the dragon with one movement of His right hand.

I watched as the glassy film over both the man's eyes slid down his cheeks and onto the ground. He stared around him as if in tremendous shock and a look of intense horror crossed his features.

"I don't belong here . . . ," he muttered.

He stared around in shock and revulsion, then looked down and tried desperately to cover his nakedness.

Then he looked up, straight into the eyes of the Lord Jesus. He flung himself to the floor, sobbing uncontrollably in desperation, hiding his eyes from the brilliance of the Lord's presence with his forearm.

Jesus knelt next to him and gently removed his forearm from his face.

"I have fallen too far."

Jesus sighed deeply.

His look was somewhat sterner than I had seen before.

"Yes," He sighed again. "You have fallen far from My grace but never so far that My grace cannot reach you."

He was silent for a moment.

"If you want it to be so," whispered the man.

"Have mercy on me, a sinner.

"Grant me Your grace in Your infinite mercy.

"Grant Your grace to me, the worst of sinners.

"I want it – I want it to be so."

Jesus sighed and gently cradled the man's head in His arms and held him as a mother would in His arms, rocking, rocking him gently.

Mucus flowed with the man's tears onto Jesus' hands, but still Jesus rocked him as a babe, looking on him with unimaginable tenderness and a great sorrow.

Loving him.

Oh, how greatly He loved him.

I watched, tears streaming down my own cheeks.

"How immense is Your grace . . . ."

"'I did not come for the lovely," Jesus answered quietly, still rocking the man in His arms.

"I came to save those who are lost.

"I came to bind up the brokenhearted.

"I came for those so bound in their sin, they cannot get free.

"I came for those lost in their pride and their delusion.

"I came for the unlovely.

"All these I died for on the cross.

"All these who have fallen so far from My grace, I yearn for.

"Tell My Church to go out into the highways.

"Go out into the byways and to save that which is lost.

"Tell My Church that many of those who are the most unlovely of today shall be My Father's champions of tomorrow.

"Tell My Church that those who have been forgiven much, love much."

Jesus rose.

With the man leaning heavily on Him, together they walked through the gate out into the garden where the winds started to blow across the man's countenance, and although his eyes were still closed, his entire expression exuded a deep, unfathomable peace.

"Much will he suffer for My sake in his restitution process. But he shall overcome.

"And he shall raise up many, many others who have been where he has been.

"Come, My child – there is something else you must see."

I followed Jesus' gaze over to where far in the distance seemed to be a brightly colored carnival tent and a garden party.

"No, *there* . . . ," Jesus pointed further to the right in the direction of a long, Spartan, white building.

"It looks like a sanatorium?" I asked.

Jesus nodded.

"Let us walk . . . ."

THE WOUNDED WARRIORS

I followed Jesus step by step as He continued to walk down the valley in the direction of the brightly colored marquee.

The tent flaps were wide open, and inside the marquee were rows and rows of beautifully laid tables, as though in preparation for a magnificent garden party.

As people were alerted to Jesus' approach, they began lining up outside the marquee.

They seemed to be in great anticipation of their honored guest, patting their hair, smoothing their jackets, earnestly intent that not a hair was out of place. They all, without exception, seemed to be wearing their 'Sunday best' in preparation for this great occasion.

As we drew nearer, I could see that the tables were laden with silver platters of exquisitely iced cakes. There was gleaming silverware on each table.

I turned to look at Jesus and gasped.

Where His head had previously been bare, He now wore the jeweled crown of a great King.

He motioned me to join Him as He entered into a white mother-of-pearl carriage drawn by eight magnificent white stallions.

Again He beckoned for me to join Him, so I climbed in beside Him.

On the opposite seat of the carriage was a huge jeweled chest that was bound and closed.

"*This* is My Father's chest," Jesus said.

"He has commissioned Me today to perform an affair of state.

"Today, I will hand out His medals to some of the most esteemed sons and daughters of My Father's kingdom."

"So that is why they are all dressed in their Sunday finest . . . ," I thought. It now made sense.

Jesus was about to hand out medals, so it was to be a bit like the Queen's garden parties.

As we neared the marquee, there was an uproarious cry of delight and welcome from the men and women outside.

A welcoming committee in ceremonial dress stood ahead of the rest of the people.

But, as we drew nearer to the marquee, the horses kept at their steady pace and did not seem to be slowing down.

We passed the ceremonial committee.

"Shouldn't we stop?" I asked Jesus. "And go to the garden party they have prepared for you?"

Jesus sat silent, His eyes fixed straight ahead.

"Today is an extraordinary day in the courts of Heaven.

"My Father's medals are to be awarded," He reiterated.

I sank back in the plush carriage seat.

Obviously we would be turning back in the direction of the marquee at any moment.

But as I turned, the marquee grew smaller and smaller on the horizon, the thousands of people dressed in all their finery appeared to be whispering amongst themselves in bewilderment.

"When will we turn around?" I asked innocently.

Jesus was quiet.

The carriage continued on down the valley for some time until the unattractive white sanatorium we had seen in the distance came fully into view.

Finally the carriage came to a halt.

Waiting outside the sanatorium to greet us was only a handful of people.

They seemed exhausted and somewhat harassed, dressed in the working uniforms of doctors and nurses.

Their uniforms were stained with the tasks of the day.

Jesus' face was radiant.

He walked straight over to a man who seemed to be the head of the sanatorium and embraced him long in deep affection, as though he was an old friend.

Jesus looked at him questioningly.

"We have saved many ...." Tears fell unashamedly down the doctor's cheeks.

"But some have suffered severe wounds."

There was a loud noise and I turned as a large truck with a red cross arrived outside the sanatorium.

The head of the sanatorium spoke a few more whispered words to Jesus, then immediately our greeting party disbanded.

All ran at top speed to assist the dying and the wounded.

Jesus turned to me.

"My child – you stand on Holy Ground.

"What you see here is a place which receives those straight from the front lines of My army.

"Few hear about them.

"But they are greatly esteemed and greatly loved by My Father and the heavenly witnesses.

"These are My children who look after the dying and the wounded. They are often over run by sheer need ... but that is changing ...."

Suddenly it was as though my eyes were opened, and I saw that the sanatorium was literally surrounded by battalions of angels.

Many were healing angels and wore red crosses on their arms.

Others were warring angels.

Others were the guardian angels of those who were inside the sanatorium being tended to.

An angel reverently removed the jeweled chest from the carriage and bowed deeply to Jesus.

Jesus nodded.

They entered the sanatorium. I followed.

Thousands of the wounded were lined up in unending rows and rows of beds.

Most were quiet and obviously recovering.

A small number, who had just arrived, were screaming in pain and terror from all they had experienced.

Jesus walked immediately to the sound of the loudest scream of agony.

As soon as the soldier saw Him, he quieted instantly in relief.

"Thank you . . . ," Jesus whispered, looking into the terrified soldier's eyes with immense love and deep compassion.

Jesus sat on the floor next to the soldier and tenderly laid His hand on the wounded soldier's head.

"The greatest terror for a soldier who has been wounded in the front-line end-time battle is that of abandonment," Jesus said softly.

He closed the soldier's eyes and instantly the soldier fell into a deep and restful sleep.

"You are here to give them the medals?" I asked.

"Not the people at the marquee?"

Jesus' face was radiant.

"I am here to give them the *Father's* medals.

"Some of these, My generals, have suffered much. Much for Me and for My Father's sake.

"Many of them have held off the enemy from destroying thousands of lives.

"They have fought the enemy on the front lines.

"They have taken much enemy land and territory.

"They have stood with great courage in Our power, even when they themselves were exhausted and suffering.

"Through their great valor and fortitude, they have reclaimed many of the high places of the enemy but often at tremendous cost to themselves and their families.

"Because of their great courage as forerunners, some of them have attracted the enemy's great wrath and a violent assault was launched against their bodies, their minds, their souls. They have stood and endured for many months and years."

BUT WE COMMEND OURSELVES IN EVERY WAY AS [TRUE] SERVANTS OF GOD: THROUGH GREAT ENDURANCE, IN TRIBULATION AND SUFFERING, IN HARDSHIPS AND PRIVATIONS, IN SORE STRAITS AND CALAMITIES,

IN BEATINGS, IMPRISONMENTS, RIOTS, LABORS, SLEEPLESS WATCHING, HUNGER;

BY INNOCENCE AND PURITY, KNOWLEDGE AND SPIRITUAL INSIGHT, LONG-SUFFERING AND PATIENCE, KINDNESS, IN THE HOLY SPIRIT, IN UNFEIGNED LOVE;

BY [SPEAKING] THE WORD OF TRUTH, IN THE POWER OF GOD, WITH THE WEAPONS OF RIGHTEOUSNESS FOR THE RIGHT HAND [TO ATTACK] AND FOR THE LEFT HAND [TO DEFEND];

AMID HONOR AND DISHONOR; IN DEFAMING AND EVIL REPORT AND IN PRAISE AND GOOD REPORT. [WE ARE BRANDED] AS DECEIVERS (IMPOSTORS), AND [YET VINDICATED AS] TRUTHFUL AND HONEST.

(2 Corinthians 6:4–8)

Jesus hesitated. He looked around at the wounded lying all around Him.

"But they will heal," He sighed.

"My Father's eye is eternally upon them.

"My Holy Spirit, the Comforter, is continually ministering to them.

"*These* are our generals. Our warriors. Many are unknown in the corridors of Earth.

"They have fought the enemy to their own great cost."

Jesus nodded and immediately two angels unbound the chest.

Jesus removed an incredibly exquisite medal of gold and diamonds, and then walked over to the corner of the sanatorium where a man laid quietly, trembling in despair, tears seeping from his eyes.

"This soldier has shown untold valor.

"He has seen many, many things.

"He has taken many of the enemy's high places and in doing so has greatly suffered in the battle for My sake."

Jesus leaned over and kissed the soldier gently – oh, so gently on his head, then gently pinned the diamond and gold medal to the left of his heart.

Slowly the man opened his eyes.

He stared at Jesus and a tremendous light infused his features.

"This medal brings restoration.

"Restoration of all that has been lost.

"Restoration of joy.

"Restoration of hope.

"Restoration of his ministry.

"Restoration of his family.

"Restoration of his backslidden children.

"Restoration of his finances.

"Restoration of his body.

"Restoration of his mind.

"Everything that seemed to be lost is being restored."

[WE ARE TREATED] AS UNKNOWN AND IGNORED [BY THE WORLD],
AND [YET WE ARE] WELL-KNOWN AND RECOGNIZED [BY GOD AND HIS
PEOPLE]; AS DYING, AND YET HERE WE ARE ALIVE; AS CHASTENED BY
SUFFERING AND [YET] NOT KILLED;

  AS GRIEVED AND MOURNING, YET [WE ARE] ALWAYS REJOICING;

AS POOR [OURSELVES, YET] BESTOWING RICHES ON MANY; AS HAVING
NOTHING, AND [YET IN REALITY] POSSESSING ALL THINGS.

(2 Corinthians 6:9–10)

Jesus held the man's hands tightly in His and turned to me.

"The men and women, you witnessed outside the marquee? They should be here with us today celebrating these very ones that lie wounded within these walls.

"But they are so caught up in their own worlds that they do not recognize many of them, My child.

"My Church still too often places great stock in the outward trappings of both men and women."

Jesus raised His hand and instantly we were transported into the center of the marquee where now hundreds of the fashionably dressed men and women were sipping tea and eating cake.

The festive atmosphere had now been replaced by a disgruntled air.

One woman in ceremonial dress pursed her lips and shook her head.

"Tut-tut, to *think* that the Lord would actually visit *that* place!"

A man dressed in ceremonial robes and with what looked like a mayor's chain around his neck agreed.

"They are only there because they didn't have enough faith," he muttered. "If they had exercised *any faith at all* they would never have been wounded in the first place . . . ."

"And probably unforgiveness . . . ," muttered another.

"Bitterness."

"*Pride* . . . ." A man with a large head sipped at his tea.

"Pride comes before a fall. There are no wounds without a landing place. Their walk with the Lord must have been *deeply* flawed.

"Look at *us* – *we* have *no* wounds!"

There was a loud murmuring of agreement from the crowd.

"*We* have *no* wounds . . . ."

All at once we were back in the sanatorium.

The Lord was deeply grieved.

"Again, I say they should be here. Caring for and loving those who have received great wounds in this end-time battle. They should be binding up their wounds and washing their feet. Praying them back to full strength. Caring for their families. But instead they . . . ."

"They drink tea . . . ," I finished the sentence for the Lord.

"Yes," said the Lord wryly.

"They drink tea and judge their brethren in the safety of their own four walls.

"If they had viewed the persecution and suffering and the assaults on My own disciples after My resurrection first hand, they may have judged them too as having little faith . . .

"All except John the beloved were martyred."

The Lord sighed, and then held a sobbing soldier's hand tightly in His own.

"My Father ordained this man as one of His great evangelists: an evangelist to this generation.

"He was saved by My own hand from deep in the world.

"He took me at My word and went and preached in the highways and the byways of the nations. He launched many apostolic works.

"Entire nations were touched by his ministry. By his sacrifice . . . ."

Jesus gently placed His hand on the bandages on the man's torso.

"He has toiled day and night for My gospel, unseen by most, facing untold persecution.

"Whole nations have been touched by his ministry.

"Most of the wounds of those you see lying here have been received from persecution and the violent assault of the enemy, but there are others who are suffering wounds. Their plight is also deeply grieving to Me and My Father. Come follow Me."

THE VEIL OF SHAME

I suddenly found myself standing with Jesus, back at the same marquee with the disgruntled tea party still in progress.

The difference was that this time Jesus was not visible to the party-goers.

And this time we were standing *inside* the marquee.

"Over there."

Jesus pointed towards the very back of the marquee.

I followed the direction of His finger.

Barely visible, almost right at the back of the marquee, hung a strange, gossamer-like veil.

I could vaguely discern the outline of many shadowy figures behind the veil, as it was woven in such a manner that, no matter where I stood, the veil completely obscured my view of any of the figures behind it.

"Who is behind there?" I asked the Lord.

He sighed.

Not in exasperation, but rather the long, suffering sigh of a loving parent whose children were dull of understanding.

"My brothers and sisters. *Your* brothers and sisters."

He hesitated.

"My Father's children. His beloved sons and daughters sit behind the veil."

I frowned.

I could not for the life of me see a way in.

"How do they come *out?*"

"They don't come out. My Church, bound in its present shackles to religion, have placed them under this veil.

"And as long as they continue to be influenced by the religious and pharisaical spirit of the age, many of My Father's children will stay bound and trapped under the veil you see."

I moved nearer.

Now that I was closer, the veil seemed extremely heavy.

It was almost like the heavy stage curtains in a theater, except that it was woven intricately, almost like the gossamer of a spider's web.

And it was a sickly grey color.

"It is the *Veil of Shame*," Jesus explained, deeply grieved.

"My Father and I came to set the captives free."

"They have been bound in the veil of shame by the enemy?" I asked.

"Not exactly."

Again Jesus was unendingly patient.

"They have been placed under the veil of shame by My Church, by their brothers and their sisters. Look."

We turned to where a compassionate-looking young girl had risen to her feet and had started to walk towards the veil.

Immediately a group of older, very wise-looking men and women caught her by the arm.

"You can't go in there. Keep yourself from being tainted."

At these words one of the few flickering lights burning behind the veil of shame was extinguished.

Jesus shook His head.

"Follow Me."

He walked straight through the veil and I followed. Suddenly we were inside an enormous, cave-like web.

Hundreds of people sat hunched and hopeless at tables.

Others were hiding in the shadows.

Still others were huddled together in the darkest corners.

ALL of them were swathed in the same sticky, intricately woven, spider-like gossamer from head to toe.

"The more they hide from the light, the more bound they become.

"If My Church would just stop condemning these people and guide them out into the light and tear away this veil of shame that they themselves have placed upon these ones, they would be swiftly liberated. It is the Church that has created this veil."

"You mean the established Church?"

"No." The Lord was quite definite.

"I mean *My Church*.

"Yes, the religious spirit has targeted these ones with a vengeance.

"With shame, guilt and eventually despair."

Jesus made His way to a young man huddled in the darkest corner.

He hid his head from Jesus.

Another girl was smoking under the veil, trying to hide from the people in the marquee.

Another was popping different medications for anxiety, then trying to hide the bottle.

Yet another was hiding bottles of gin.

While another was stashing pornographic magazines into the darkest corner he could find.

"Now watch."

Instantly, as Jesus raised His hand, a searing light illuminated the entire marquee.

Then Jesus walked towards a girl who was chain-smoking.

As soon as she saw Him, she crushed the cigarette packet in her hand and made a vain attempt to hide it from the Lord.

Tenderly, He unclenched her fingers and removed the cigarettes from her grasp.

He laid them on the table.

There was a horrified gasp from the rest of the marquee.

He bent His head to hers, took her face in His hands and whispered to her for a long while. Tears streamed down her cheeks.

She flung her arms around Him.

"Thank You, thank You."

Jesus stood.

"See her *heart?* A heart of generosity and kindness."

He moved His hand and everyone fell silent.

There was the same girl, her arms around the homeless, loving them, arranging shelter for them and feeding them.

Jesus looked down at the pack of cigarettes.

"You condemn her for smoking.

"Behind her back you criticize her and have ostracized her.

"You have covered and ensnared her in your veil of shame.

"But it is *your* veil of shame, not hers."

A heroin addict ran into Jesus' arms and buried her head into His chest.

Tenderly, He stroked her hair.

"Who will walk with her and love her into freedom?"

A man walked towards them from the marquee. He bowed before Jesus.

"I will help her. I used to be an addict. Forgive me for judging her in her weakness. *I* will walk with her."

Next, Jesus laid His hand on the man who was popping myriad anxiety meds in desperation.

He immediately stopped shaking.

A fleeting pain passed over Jesus' features.

"I don't condemn you, child. Remember in Gethsemane, when I sweated drops of blood?"

His voice became very soft.

"I remember what it is to be traumatized by fear . . . ."

Tears streamed down the man's cheeks.

With infinite compassion, Jesus drew the sobbing man into His arms, his body wracked with sobs.

Jesus raised His head to the onlookers in the marquee.

"I came to set the captive free."

Jesus' tears mingled with the man's tears.

"Never judge nor condemn those who walk in paths you have never trodden.

"I came not for those who are well, but for those in need of a physician.

"I came to bind up the brokenhearted.

"Each of these you see here today has a fissure in their soul from the enemy. In their desperation of heart, they have tried to fill the unhealed pain, the trauma, the vacuum in their souls with all the things you see beneath the veil of shame today.

"Drugs, hard alcohol, prescription medications, pornography – these are only symptoms.

"Symptoms of unhealed wounds and deep-rooted pain"

BLESSED BE THE GOD AND FATHER OF OUR LORD JESUS CHRIST, THE FATHER OF SYMPATHY (PITY AND MERCY) AND THE GOD [WHO IS THE SOURCE] OF EVERY COMFORT (CONSOLATION AND ENCOURAGEMENT).
(2 Corinthians 1:3)

"Our Holy Spirit is the Comforter. My Father Himself is the God of *all* Comfort. *All* consolation.

"If My Church had wrapped them in her arms and had poured out unconditional love and discipled these ones with a fervent pure love from My Father and taught them how to use My Word.

"In only a short space of time, *every* symptom, *every* habit would have been shed from their lives like a cocoon."

"But, instead, yes, many of My Church teach them My Word, and yet in their self-righteousness, place a straitjacket of guilt and of shame upon the very ones whose freedom will only be found in the light.

"My Father is the Great Physician.

"He is *never offended by the symptom*.

"His gentle surgeon's hand goes straight to the root cause, to the heart of every man and every woman."

Jesus raised His hands and tore the heavy curtain in two, laying it on the ground.

"When the curtain in the Holy of Holies was rent in two, when I died on the Cross, the veil of shame was destroyed."

Those inside started to run from the light. But suddenly people from all over the marquee were standing, repenting, running towards the veil and surrounding them with love.

And one by one, I saw the sticky, web-like gossamer veils begin to fall off each one like a cocoon.

Then the marquee disappeared from view.

I raised my gaze. Far in the distance, I could see a battle raging.

I saw warriors fighting on the front lines.

I saw soldiers stationed on the high places, looking out for the enemy.

They were stationed at intervals on the top of mountains and the high places.

"Who are they, Lord?" I asked.

"They are the end-time intercessors; they are the army's watchmen on the walls."

"But there are huge *gaps* all across there." I pointed to where there were no watchmen at all.

Suddenly I saw a huge battalion of the enemy's camp marching towards a solitary watchman left on the mountains. They took careful aim. The watchman fell.

I knew this was not good.

The Lord pointed downward to a group of soldiers who were hunched over what looked like communication tools – radios and transmitters.

"Oh, no!" I uttered. There was a huge battalion of the enemy coming over the hill towards them. A moment later they were blown up.

I looked back to the front line.

THE FRONT LINE

The vast battle plateau stretched as far as the eye could see.

It was strange.

Something seemed amiss.

I watched the company of generals that stood shield to shield holding the front line.

They were obviously experienced warriors.

Steady and strong. Their dress was almost like the Vikings. Their faces were set like flint. I saw that on their shields was written APOSTLES.

But there was something amiss.

Finally I realized what it was.

It was the fact that although it was the front line, it seemed unnaturally quiet. There were a few skirmishes that the apostles easily put down.

They kept marching steadily forward.

But where on Earth was the *heat of the battle*?

I could hear bloodthirsty, curdling screams of war in the distance.

I could hear the chilling sounds of carnage.

But for the life of me I couldn't see where they were coming from.

Far to the right was a second company of warriors.

They seemed far more vocal, almost flamboyant. They were also moving forward.

They looked as though they were in kilts, Scottish ceremonial war dress, with many playing the bagpipes.

They were the company of EVANGELISTS.

Their swords were flourished.

Once again they were marching forward with flair, very steadily, but strangely, in a completely different direction to the apostles.

In fact, the apostles and the evangelists were so independent of each other it seemed as though they were fighting *separate* wars.

Then I saw the carnage ahead of me.

Some of the watchmen were terribly wounded.

But the worst hit of all were the prophets and the seers.

No sooner had they regrouped than there was yet another onslaught from the enemy. In fact, almost the entire onslaught of the enemy's forces seemed in this season aimed at the army's intelligence and communication.

The prophets, the seers and the end-times company of intercessors who were rising.

The enemy well knew that their gifting was different from those of the sturdy apostles swinging their mighty weapons, rushing into war.

These three battalions were the Father's supreme intelligence corps.

Highly attuned to the strategy and blueprints of Heaven and possessing the accurate discernment of the enemy's strategies and war plans.

In fact, many of these prophets, seers and intercessors had been to the enemy's own war rooms undetected.

And were *devastating* to the enemy's plans.

Stopping them at every turn.

They were greatly hated and feared by the enemy.

I watched as a great company of the enemy's front-liners – powers and principalities – came out of a secret war council.

Their generals led a great company of Satan's fiercest and violent warriors in their company. I saw a violent company headed up by Infirmity.

Then a second blood-thirsty company of the damned holding up a blood-dripping banner that read: WAR AGAINST THE SAINTS.

Then I heard a strange cacophonic sound, almost like a huge battalion of bats whirring.

It was called demonic interference.

As one, they rode past the apostles and charged upon the hidden intelligence corps.

The apostles were still marching steadily to the sound of war drums, but many seemed oblivious to these contingents of the enemy.

Then I saw a different company of apostles who seemed to be in excellent contact with a company of the communications and intelligence forces.

The apostles turned and immediately marshaled their forces against the enemy who was overrun quickly and efficiently.

It was evident that the prophets and seers were a vital part of these apostles' structure, as the apostles were completely integral to the prophets, seers and intercessors.

My eye was drawn to a particular section of this army where a pastor was being held aloft in an ornately carved litter. The soldiers on foot around him were bloodied, weary and battle-worn, but were running to serve the pastor as though their lives depended upon it.

And I saw the words POWER and CONTROL.

And I knew the Lord was very grieved.

But as I continued to watch, the Lord drew my attention to another battalion where the pastors were marching alongside their battalions.

They were bloodied and weary but exhilarated.

Their exhilaration came from their tireless, sacrificial tending to their flocks.

They bound up the broken-hearted and the wounded, sparing no thoughts to their own wounds or weariness.

Caring for them.

Communicating with them as a *treasured family*.

I saw many, *many* pastors like this.

Then I watched as new mantles – apostolic mantles – appeared over these faithful pastors.

The Lord Jesus said, "For those of My pastors who have laid down their own lives to feed My flock and protect My sheep – there is a new season arising. For in this present and coming season, many, many of those who My Father has found faithful will now rise in this latter season of My Church age with a new apostolic mantle."

I watched as thousands of these pastors, now bearing strong apostolic mantles of great authority, rose and took their places in the Front Line.

Out of their mouths came the sword of the Spirit and two things inhabited their speech:

The grace of God and the love of the Father

However, many others of the pastors and apostles had not, in this present Church Age, completely embraced and incorporated the prophets, seers and intercessors into their ranks.

Instead, the intelligence corps seemed to act as an independent unit.

Receiving and disseminating information anywhere it was welcomed and received.

The Lord drew my attention to the watchmen far above the army on the walls. There were now very few still standing.

Many had been overpowered and flung from the walls.

There were many, many gaps as far as the eye could see.

I knew instantly that these were the end-times intercessors.

Now there seemed to be an incredibly strong working relationship between the intercessors, the prophets and the seers.

In fact, these three battalions worked in such unity and so smoothly together that if the apostles, evangelists and pastors had actually decided to incorporate them into their battle plan, instead of marching in independence, they would have received absolutely vital intelligence and communication that could have at least halved the battle time and would have shown them blueprints of the traps and mines set for them.

Saving many, many warriors' lives.

Providing them with precise co-ordinates.

However, the *shocking* thing was that many of the apostles seemed to feel absolutely *no* necessity to collaborate with the intelligence and communication groups whatsoever.

A section of the apostles and prophets who *were* collaborating seemed to be pulling each other in opposite directions, shouting above the battle fray about differences in timing and coordinates and eventually, both totally frustrated, each went back to their independence again vowing they were unable to work together.

And even worse – some evangelists seemed to be completely independent of both the apostles *and* the prophets.

And a great company of the pastors were marching about a mile behind both.

Whereas the apostles seemed almost unaware or dismissive of the prophets, seers and intercessors, it appeared that many of the pastors were actually *mistrusting* of the prophets and the seers. And the intercessors.

It was as though the intercessors, who were actually one of the most *vital* end-times' battalions, were being almost completely ignored by the *entire* army as an afterthought.

But at the same time, some of the prophets were also *fiercely* independent and refusing to come under the apostles' control.

It seemed to be a raging battle of wills between the apostles and the prophets, let alone between the Church army and the enemy!

I sensed that the prophets and the seers were like a godly M-16 or God's counter-terrorism unit. Their base camp was positioned far back on the battlefield. The apostles were the Jack Bauers taking the kingdom of darkness by force. But unlike the TV program *24*, the communication lines between the apostolic Jack Bauers and the prophet seer intercessors in the counter-terrorism base unit were *cut*.

I sensed the Lord Jesus behind me.

He sighed.

"It is hard for some of My leaders to change . . . ."

"The end-times battle will only be won by each and every battalion operating in its exact function and structure.

"It is only when honor reigns among My Body – when each views and treats each as better than themselves. Preferring one another in love.

"But My sons and daughters all over the Earth *are rising*.

"They are rising and are moving into a lifestyle of the Royal Law of Love."

VOLUME THREE

THE THRONE ROOM

I stood, utterly transfixed by the cascading waves of glory.

Waves and waves of literal, luminous, white glory cascaded from the throne down upon the inhabitants of the Throne Room – until the entire assembly seemed to be bathed in the glimmering cocoon of soft white fire.

And then the silence fell.

How silence could fall like that, I did not understand, but it felt literally as though I could hear the very silence in the Throne Room falling.

And in that silence was the *glory* and the *majesty* and the *wisdom* and the *power* and the *holy fear* of Almighty God.

And in that silence was the *love* and the *omnipotence* and the *mercy* and the *infinite compassions* of the Father from whom all fatherhood had been named.

And still the silence fell.

A silence unlike anything I had ever known on Earth.

It was silence and yet the silence was filled with the manifold utterances of the Holy Spirit, to each and every heart and each and every soul.

I could not see the color of the leaves of the pages of the Book of Life, because each leaf shone with such luminosity that, from the sides of the book, such a blazing light exuded, the book itself was barely visible.

And I sensed from the Angelic Host such a dread and a wonder.

The absolute *wonder* of what was in these pages.

Then the silence changed in its atmosphere.

And a holy dread descended.

It seemed as though the holy terror of the Lord Himself, of the great I AM, of the Ancient of Days, fell across the chamber like a thick, falling shroud.

As one, the entire chamber fell to their knees and on their faces – prostrate as the glory of the Father grew in intensity from the throne.

The angels fell prostrate before the One who sat on the throne.

And multiple millions fell trembling and prostrate, and still the holy terror fell. Fell.

Fell.

Even falling as the dusk used to fall on Earth.

I could not look up, but stayed on my face, trembling.

And the angelic shofars blew and a voice declared – "Open the Book!"

Still trembling, I watched from the floor as Jesus slowly moved towards the Father's throne.

And then in front of me the figure of Jesus Christ transformed to the figure of a lamb that was slain with seven horns and seven eyes.

I recognized this lamb as the Lamb that opened the book of the seven seals mentioned in Revelation. Then I heard proclaimed the words from Revelation:

"You are worthy to take the scroll and to open its seals, because you were slain, and with your blood you purchased men for God from every tribe and language and people and nation. You have made them to be a kingdom and priests to serve our God, and they will reign on the earth. Worthy is the Lamb, who was slain, to receive power and wealth and wisdom and strength and honor and glory and praise!"

And the holy glory of God saturated the chamber.

And the slain Lamb transformed back into the person of Jesus Christ.

Tears ran down Jesus' face as He knelt in front of His beloved Father.

And I knew that this book, HIS Book, the Book of the Lamb, was the *greatest* gift in the universe that He now presented to the One who was His all in all, Creator of the Universes and Galaxies, the Ancient of Days, the MOST HIGH, His beloved Father.

Then Jesus spoke.

"I, the Lamb, that was sacrificed for the sins of the world – I, Your only begotten Son, present the Lamb's Book of Life."

Waves of glory emanated from the place where the Father sat and somehow I could sense that He was moved.

Moved beyond comprehension, remembering the sacrifice of His only begotten, beloved Son but also deeply, ***deeply*** moved by what He knew lay *within* the pages of the Book.

For the Father knew that what lay between the pages of the Book of the slain Lamb, was the most precious and esteemed gift in the universe and every universe beyond.

The precious gift that brought the Angelic Host to their knees, weeping.

The precious gift that was the love of ordinary sons and daughters of Earth, who had received the sacrifice of Jesus Christ, His Son, and been reconciled to the Father for eternity.

And the Father knew well that so many, *many* of these ones had been born into obscurity and frailty.

Had struggled with their own set of weaknesses and failings which so easily beset them.

Had many times on Earth cried such desperate tears, clinging to Him only by faith, seeing dimly through a glass through which they could only see darkly.

Yet *still* they had kept the faith.

Still they had believed.

Even when they had failed Him.

Even when they forsook Him and set their mind on earthly things, they would run back to Him, even as a little child, and so the God of all compassion had taken them up and comforted them, even as a mother comforts her babe.

For surely the Father of Compassion knew and remembered how they were formed.

For He well remembered that they were dust, and oh, how, the Father *loved* these ones.

AS A FATHER HAS COMPASSION ON HIS CHILDREN,

SO THE LORD HAS COMPASSION ON THOSE WHO FEAR HIM;

FOR HE KNOWS HOW WE ARE FORMED,

HE REMEMBERS THAT WE ARE DUST.

(Psalm 103:13–14 NIV)

For He would stop Heaven for the sound of one of His children worshipping Him behind closed doors.

All Heaven would stop in its wake at the command of the Father.

And every sacrifice that a son or daughter of Earth had made for Him and for the proclamation of His gospel was recorded.

Every act of worship in the secret place behind closed doors that no man ever knew, had been faithfully recorded by Heaven.

Every act of unselfishness not known or seen by man was recorded.

Every act of perseverance and fortitude in the face of persecution and opposition by wicked men, or the forces of hell, was recorded.

Every soul-winning action or initiative conducted from a pure motive, for pure love of the Father and His Son, was recorded.

Every besetting sin, struggled against and overcome, was recorded.

Every act of repentance, every act of joy, every conversation with the Father, the Son and the Holy Spirit was recorded for posterity.

And all lay within the pages of this Book.

That the Father would read for eternity.

Then Jesus smiled, a radiant smile, and the Father's hand appeared out of the white glory.

He opened the enormous Book of Life.

And Heaven waited.

Then the Father spoke a name.

And in the Father's voice was the infinite love and compassion and a depth of tenderness of the Father of all fathers – and in His voice was healing and understanding and a total embracing that was so very, very rare to be found upon the Earth as we had known it .

And, as the Father spoke that name, Jesus' gaze fell out of all assembled in the Throne Room immediately to that one.

THE FATHER'S FRIEND

*J*esus walked towards a figure surrounded by light in one of the rows near the front. A woman stepped out into the nave to meet Him. It was as though the entire assembly drew a breath.

For this woman wore an aura of holiness and authority and power as would befit a great regent – a great queen of Earth. I could not see her face; her head was covered by a veil.

Then I watched, stunned as the angels fell before her.

Jesus bowed in honor to her.

She continued alone up the nave, straight towards the throne and the brilliance of white light.

In my earthly mindset, I became uneasy, thinking at any moment surely she should stop or surely some angelic being would stop her in her stead, but she continued walking towards the throne.

She walked directly into the brilliance of light into the center of where the Father's outline was dimly, dimly visible, until her entire form disappeared.

"Who *is* she?" I asked in awe.

Jesus smiled tenderly at me and looked after her, deeply moved.

"She is My Father's friend," he whispered.

Jesus raised His hand and the vista in front of us changed.

I watched as a plain, black-haired babe was born to a single mother in Scotland during the First World War.

"She was placed into an orphanage. She was put into service at the age of ten.

"Raped by the man of the house at the age of fourteen. She cried so many tears of anger, rage and helplessness in her small, dark, cold room. She had a great calling – a calling to Us," said the Lord softly. "She would have come to My Father much sooner if some of our children had been more sensitive and less concerned with their own four walls and needs.

"She married at fifteen. Had nine children. She was regularly beaten by her alcoholic husband. Finally he left her, penniless."

I nodded and Jesus motioned to me to continue watching.

"I watched as she worked day and night, scrubbing and cleaning to keep her children, growing weaker and weaker through the years, eventually losing her health. I saw her children abandon her, breaking her heart and she was eventually placed in a workhouse."

Jesus smiled and nodded.

"You are wondering what place she holds with Us, when we held no place in her life for so many years?

"She was left to die," Jesus said. "Unloved and abandoned."

I followed His gaze back to the woman in the workhouse.

"Finally, beloved, she was visited in the workhouse by one of Our faithful servants who told her about Me. She was given one small New Testament, and even in her frail and dying state, she clung to whatever words she could. She began to call My name day and night, day and night.

"In her utter desperation and fear and desolation of soul, she cried out to Us."

Tears welled up in Jesus' eyes.

"And so, beloved, her plaintive cries reached Us right here in this throne room. I rushed to her bedside. She was in the final stages of dying, and she could see clearly into the spirit realm. And she grasped My robe. 'Oh, heal me, sweet Jesus!'

"And in that moment she reached out her hand to Mine. 'Help thou mine unbelief.'"

"She was healed," I said in awe, watching as she grew stronger and then saw her leaving the workhouse and working once more as a maid, now healthy and strong. And, oh – she was forever – forever changed.

"This is all wonderful, Lord," I said, "such a salvation in the most dire of circumstances, but I still don't understand how she could . . . could . . . ."

Jesus smiled patiently. "How she could walk straight to the Father's throne and nestle in His breast in front of the entire assembly of Heaven?"

I nodded and followed Jesus' gaze.

The woman knelt in her tiny attic bedroom, her hands raised, her face shining in complete and utter adoration, worshipping the Father.

"You are glorious, glorious, all glorious . . . Holy, Holy . . . You are beautiful . . . , " she was uttering. Then she would blow Him kisses, and lean her head on His breast like a small child with its mother, and always, *always* she would sing love songs to the Father.

And then I saw the scenario change, and I watched her worship and child-like adoration move in a flame of fire, like a huge flame of white incense through the roof, through the skies of Earth and through the heavens, and the white flame came up on the altar before the Father's throne.

And then I saw an incredible thing.

The Father was in counsel with Jesus and the Holy Spirit and all around the Councils of Heaven were in session. But now the Father raised His hand, His only focus being the sweet, sweet burning-white, incense-like flame that burned on the altar.

And it was as though He grasped Jesus' hand in gratitude again for the terrible sacrifice on Golgotha. And the incense was brought to Him and the Father took it and brought it to His chest and it became the woman, and she was there in the Father's embrace, kissing His face and hands and laying her head against His chest.

And how deeply He was moved.

How profoundly He was touched by her great love and adoration for Him.

Then I saw her back in her bedroom. It was around 3:00 a.m. and she was deeply asleep. And I saw the Father yearning for her fellowship, for she would spend most nights talking to Him. Not praying, not petitioning, but sharing with Him her most intimate secrets as a father and a daughter, and in turn, He would share His most intimate secrets of His bride and His Son. And in turn, she would pray and she would intercede for the Church.

But this night, she was asleep.

But how the Father yearned for her, and I saw angels dispatched. And they came up the stairs to her bedroom and gently, gently they woke her.

And the Father fellowshipped with His beloved.

And each night, in her small, sparsely furnished bedroom, she would lay a dinner place for the Father and sit and share her innermost secrets with Him.

The vista changed again, and instantly I was standing outside the most incredible building. It seemed to me more like a palace than a mansion.

The building was created of pure white marble with flecks of delicate pink, surrounded by glorious parkland. Deer and unicorns were roaming the park. Exotic peacocks and pheasants and types of birds with golden beaks and pale turquoise feathers were feeding their young. There must have been thousands of the most exquisite roses of every type and every color weighing down each bush; roses even climbed the palace walls.

I gasped in amazement.

"Who lives in there? It's like Buckingham Palace."

"There is someone My Father wants you to meet."

A slender young woman with milky white skin and gleaming waist-length black hair sat in the garden at the far side of the mansion, about a hundred yards away. Then I saw Him.

The Father was seated on a beautifully carved stone bench, opposite the woman. Her eyes were totally fixed on His face. Transfixed by Him. Adoring Him. And He with her.

The scene was so precious; it felt as though we were intruding.

"He visits her," Jesus said softly. "My Father visits her every day at the time of Earth's dusk, as she visited Him when she lived on Earth."

"Who is she?"

Jesus looked at me with compassion for my dullness of under-standing.

The regal woman walked towards us. Jesus bowed deeply to her. He seemed deeply overcome

"I am the woman you saw in the workhouse."

She placed her hands on mine.

"You and those who stand on Earth in this present season of the Church Age are greatly loved here in Heaven. And you are greatly loved by the Father. There is nothing . . . ."

Her eyes welled up with tears that fell down her cheeks. She was greatly overcome.

"There is nothing that can compare with knowing the Father . . . ."

She turned and made her way back to the rose arbor where she was surrounded by children. She sang to them as she tended her roses.

"See how she tends the roses? With such joy, so tenderly."

"All those years on Earth, the Father knew that her greatest heart's desire was to have a tiny rose garden just to drink in the perfume of the roses."

I stared around in wonder. There must have been at least one hundred acres of rose gardens.

"In her latter days, she became quite blind; oh, but *how* she saw Him in her spirit. She used to set a place for Him at her table.

"He used to come to her, you know. My Father would leave the joy and wonders of Heaven, just for the wonder to be with her. For she loved Him so.

"The day she died on Earth, they took her body and dumped it in the pauper's grave.

"No one was there. No one cared.

"All those she had spent her life looking after were long gone.

"She arrived here within the gates of Heaven.

"My Father's was the first face that she saw. Oh, the joy! Unspeakable!

"You see, beloved, whatever the relationship My children experience with My Father while they are on the Earth, they will experience the same when they are with Him in Heaven.

"Many, many of My Father's children are so busy working *for* Him that they forget to fellowship *with* Him."

I knew that many ministers would panic at this statement.

"But they pour their lives out to preach Your gospel?"

Again the Lord smiled gently.

"The Father loves these ones intimately. Without these, surely His Kingdom would not be built in strength and in might, and they will forever be close to Him. And many of these know My Father and they are greatly prized by Him. But there is yet another place.

"For the ones who cling to Him in intimacy. For the ones who yearn to be with Him. For the ones who cover Him with kisses. And cover Him with their love at every turn.

"Many of these are My ministers also, but many are also those who on Earth live in obscurity, their deeds for My Father unnoticed by those on Earth."

"But not unnoticed by You and the Father."

Jesus nodded.

"My Father's desolation at the separation from His children was reversed at the cross. But His *joy* is His fellowship with His children. He is a Father. He is the Father after whom all fatherhood is named. And the Father loves His children. He longs to fellowship with His children, to play with His children. To laugh and dance, sing and talk with His children.

"And the Father's heart is not complete without His sons' and daughters' fellowship.

"There are many crowns, and many rewards, beloved.

"But the greatest crown and the greatest reward from the Father's hand . . . ."

Jesus smiled.

" . . . is for the Father's friends."

THE MINISTER

*A*ll at once that scene disappeared from view and I heard another name called.

Jesus walked some way down the nave of the Throne Room towards the figure that was now on his knees, trembling, his gaze fixed on Jesus Christ, unable to withdraw his gaze. Jesus held out His hand, the most incredible, wondrous smile on His face.

Tears streamed down the man's face. He shook his head from side to side.

"I failed You . . . ," he uttered.

Jesus' smile grew broader and his eyes were filled with a deep compassion and still He held out His hand.

Slowly, the man made his way through the vast unceasing crowds eventually to where Jesus was standing and threw himself down before Jesus' feet, his chest wracked with sobs, his face hidden in his hands.

Jesus looked down upon him; His own cheeks were wet with the tears that flowed. Looking upon him. Loving him.

Then Jesus turned the man to face the Father.

The man's hands dropped slowly from his face, and he seemed magnetized by the blazing light emanating from the Father's throne, without being able to stop himself – almost as though he was being drawn up the nave by an indescribable force.

He staggered up the nave until he stood in front of the throne, a look of indescribable wonder across his countenance.

And still the light blazed from the throne, but now it was softer and was coming towards the man in waves, washing, cleansing, loving his weary soul.

And still the man stared, almost paralyzed.

In wonder.

In adoration.

Transfixed by the indescribable beauty of spirit of the One who sat and adored the man.

And the man could not turn his face away from the One who sat on the throne and he held out his arms to Him.

And still the Father loved him.

Jesus walked over to the man and gently drew him away to the left side of the nave and turned his face from the throne to His.

The man flung himself on his knees and sobbed through his tears.

"My Lord – I failed You – continually towards the end of my life, I failed You. I built my own kingdom. It is all mire and clay. I would tear it all apart with my own hands, if I could just return . . . ." He broke down sobbing, unable to continue.

Jesus knelt down next to him on the chamber floor. And tenderly, oh, with such infinite tenderness, He lifted the man's face up from the floor.

"Yes, beloved son, it is true that you succumbed to many of the enemy's severest assignments against you in your latter days . . ."

Jesus did not drop His loving gaze.

"And it pleased My Father to bring you home to where we dwell, but now . . . your book is open." He clasped the man's hand gently in His.

"It is the appointed time. Let us read its pages."

Together they walked, the man leaning heavily upon Jesus who clasped him to Himself like a mother would a young, weary child. They walked to the book, the glory increasing the nearer they came to the throne until they stood together in front of the throne, opposite the enormous book with its glistening pages.

The man fell to his knees, his head bowed.

And, as Jesus spoke his name, an angel announced the day and the hour of his birth in the Earth.

And there was a great blowing of the shofars before the proclamation of his calling in the Kingdom of God.

"You were conceived in your mother's womb," the angel proclaimed, "and preordained to proclaim the Kingdom of the Most High God to prepare the way for the last generations."

A great screen filled an entire wall of the chamber, and the man's life began to play out for all to see. But it was as I looked on at the man that I reeled back with shock. Now he was completely unrecognizable.

For the entire surface of his skin was punctured by tiny, metallic-like arrows. There was also a huge arrow that was speared in towards the left side of his heart and another that had gouged his entire right side and was still bleeding.

All across the backs of his hands and his face were fresh, bleeding grazes and wounds. Boils that still festered.

Four lesser arrows, but bigger than the multitude across his body, were piercing the left side of his heart next to the larger one.

His face was dark with hopelessness.

I stood, my eyes riveted both to the man and to the walls of the chamber, and watched him being born as a babe in arms.

The entire chamber watched in silence.

I saw the love and the joy with which the Father, the Son and the Holy Spirit released this man's spirit from Heaven into the womb.

The Father rejoiced over him with singing.

Oh, how evident that he had the mark of God on his life from before his conception.

The entire chamber watched as he was born in a plainly decorated bedroom.

His mother was simple and poor, but her eyes shone with love for him and she was a praying, God-fearing woman. She had prayed for *him* – that she would give birth to a servant of the Lord and the Lord had answered her fervent desire.

His father was absent.

Jesus raised His hands, smiling down on him, and the pictures moved to when he was around eleven years old.

He stood around his mother's bed. She was dying and feeble, but laid her hands on him, clutching him to her, tears streaming down her face.

And I saw Jesus standing to her right, loving her.

Loving him.

She blessed her son, then she raised her arms to Jesus and died.

The boy was crying inconsolably.

Jesus reached out to him, but the boy could not sense Him, and I saw him clench his little fist and I saw one of the medium arrows pierce his breast with one deep lunge.

The man watched, crying. Jesus placed His hand on the man's head.

"We did not forsake you as you thought . . . ," Jesus said softly.

"Your mother's whole life was borne in poverty and hardship and frailty – she was too sick to work and could not sustain you. She had been abandoned by your father at birth and she knew she could not provide for you what you would need for your future. Her greatest desire was that you would be raised by a strong, godly minister who would love you as his own and lead you into the ministry. You were her only love on this Earth. You were her only reason to stay. But, beloved." Jesus' eyes grew misty. He raised His hand again.

The screen filled with scenes of the boy growing up in immense poverty and eventually flaunting his mother's authority and running away, ending up as a thief and a drug addict.

"If she had stayed . . . ,' Jesus looked at the man gently, "you would have broken her very heart. She would have never recovered and would have died in the workhouse, having lost her son to drugs and prison. It was time for her to be with Us."

He turned His head to His right and nodded gently. There, from one of the thrones of Heaven, walked the most noble, blonde-haired woman in her late thirties – dressed in flowing white robes, her face glowing unfettered by the cares of Earth. She ran towards him and she clasped him to her breast, stroking the head of her beloved son.

And as he wept, the arrow fell of its own accord to the floor and immediately new skin grew over the wound.

Jesus gently took the mother's hand and drew her to the side of her son.

He nodded towards the scenes now playing out.

I watched as he was taken into the home of a godly ministry family, and there the father loved him even as his own and the boy was given an excellent education and excelled in communication. He led the Christian Union at a young age and started to bring many to Christ. He then went to Bible college and trained for the full-time ministry. The scenes changed to a huge wedding as he married the family's youngest daughter, who was also a devout Christian with a soft spirit and a tender heart for the Lord. Over the years, they had four children.

God's divine will was being executed.

He went into itinerant ministry as an evangelist and I watched Jesus' face glow as the secret records of his deeds were recorded.

Heaven fell to their knees as the scene changed to him worshipping Jesus and the Father in His own private chamber – such love – such adoration of the Son and the Father – and I watched as his adoration reached up to Jesus and the Father in Heaven and they were deeply, profoundly moved by such worship and adoration coming from Earth and they manifested themselves to him.

And a great and pure ministry was birthed.

He preached the Gospel of Jesus Christ faithfully with power and signs and wonders in many, many nations as an apostle and evangelist. And many training schools were established. And many establishments were set up to feed the poor and needy. And the glory of God overshadowed the ministry.

And he raised up many, many ministers under him. And they, in turn, preached to the four corners of the Earth. And the impact of his ministry spread to the four corners of the Earth. But he remained pure, for his entire focus was the Lord.

And he did not seek to promote his own name or the name of his own endeavors. His only motive was to promote Jesus Christ.

And then I saw a great and dark assignment in the camp of the enemy being dispatched. It looked almost as though a great dark cloud was launched at his ministry and, as the cloud was launched, many of those of the enemy's camp were joined by those who had no strong foundation and were easily deceived. And a great army of opposition rose up against him and the ministry of his hands, to tear down all that had been built up.

And during this season, I saw a great and terrible arrow launched.

An arrow that carried the words LIES OF THE ENEMY, DECEPTION, and it headed straight for his heart. I watched as he deflected it with the knowledge of God and His Word and the living shed blood of Jesus. It was easily deflected because he lived in the shadow of the Most High and the arrows fell to the ground each time, even before they reached their mark. *They simply could not reach their mark*, because he lived in the *shadow of the Almighty*.

But the scenes changed and I could see that as the years went on, he grew weary.

First, it was weariness in the natural. But then times grew harder in the ministry – and I saw a small wound appear over his breastbone, like a fresh cut, and fresh blood was flowing from it.

Jesus spoke to me. "When, in the latter years of his life, a season came when he was struggling with the ministry provision and other pressing challenges of ministry, instead of looking to Me as his source, he looked to man for many answers. Eventually, as struggles grew harder, a deep feeling of abandonment started to fester in his heart. And the devil whispered to him.

"You have served Jesus Christ faithfully all these years, why is it always so hard? Why doesn't He provide for your ministry for you?"

Jesus smiled in compassion. "You see, My child. I always provide for those who serve Me, but there is also great opposition in the spirit realm that My servants must overcome. Many of My children become weary with standing on My promises and give up their faith just before they are about to receive from Heaven.

"In his later years, he was blessed with every material blessing he needed from Our hand – for how much We love those who love Us and serve Our cause."

Jesus continued. "Then in that time of severe assignment, one of his children, one very close to his heart, backslid, and the devil said, '*See – God does not keep your children after your whole life has been poured out in serving Him . . . .*'

"And again, each day, instead of coming to Me, instead of coming to My Father, his ever-present help in time of trouble, he drifted away from communion with Us through the devil's lies. And the fresh blood of the wounds of abandonment flowed freely."

Jesus turned to me.

"I was always there, beloved. At any time, if My child had just taken My hand and cried out to Me and used My Word and acted on the principles of My Word, We would have come to him. But in these latter days – the kingdom of the devil is taken by violence and the violent take it by force. Oh, My child. Tell My children, tell My beloved who fight for Me in this hour, that My army in this day and in this hour cannot be passive, for surely then the enemy will assail them.

"For it is by faith and patience that My warriors inherit the promise.

"By fortitude and courage and endurance.

"It is in the moment that My children feel most abandoned. It is in the moment that they feel most forsaken, it is in *that* moment that they must cry out to Me, cry out to My Father for My mercy, for My provision, for My ever-present help and even in that moment, they will feel My peace and I will come with My strong right hand and ward off the forces that assail them . . . ."

Jesus stopped in mid sentence and smiled with a great and tender sorrow in his eyes. " . . . I will answer *every* need. I will answer *every* prayer, no matter how dark the situation . . . ," he continued. "If . . . they will only cling to Me."

Then I saw that a second great arrow flew which read – GREAT INTIMIDATION – OPPOSITION.

And I saw a cacophony of demons who found a handful of dis-illusioned, embittered ministers who had in the past suffered from jealousy against the man. And they started to spread the word against him, saying that he did not hear God and that he was deceived.

And in this season, already having fallen to self-pity and discour-agement – instead of separating himself and setting himself apart – he had started to be overwhelmed by the cares of life and the weariness of the battle.

I winced as I saw a huge arrow come in on his blind side. It lunged straight into him with a terrible ferocity. And found its mark.

And I sensed that his greatest vulnerability at that time was that his ministry had moved from total trust in God and God's ability *alone* – to *his* ability – and now, when his gifting and his calling were questioned, instead of being secure in the fact that it was God's ministry, not his ministry, his foundations shook to their core.

And he entered the dark night of the soul.

This was an attack that in all the visions that followed seemed the most commonly occurring in this present dispensation. And also the most violent.

And somehow I was certain that if he had, at any time in that period, run to Jesus and asked Him to remove the arrow, that with just one move of His hand, Jesus Himself would have taken the arrow out. But instead, the man immediately dropped into a dark and deep depression and, as the poison from the lies of the enemy seeped through his system, it began to taint his discernment and he began to look at those close around him in ministry with the same spirit. With suspicion. With mistrust.

And Jesus said, "At any time, My child, he could have come to Me and confessed his sin – and immediately the arrow would have had no place in him. But the words of his mouth became harsh and judgmental against all those around him. First, his words were hard only against his enemies, but as the darkness in his heart grew greater, his words became harsh against his wife and his youngest son who he adored. Through the years, they, in turn, became bitter against him. Eventually, his son became bitter against Me. And slowly, because he was out of day-to-day communion with My Holy Spirit, the motives of his heart became selfishly ambitious for his own movement and the success of those who carried only his banner.

My child, many, many of My ministers even today in this generation fight these same demons, for this is the assignment that has been released in ferocity in this present Church Age. Many fall into the mire of their own self-judgments and self-pity, but those that have a tender heart towards Me, repent and run to Me. It is easy for Me to rescue these ones and I love them with an all-consuming, everlasting love, and I take out each and every arrow by My own hand, that no wound may fester there."

We turned back to the scenes of the man's life that were still playing.

I watched in horror as the tiny metallic arrows continued to pierce his skin – arrows of hatred, jealousy, self-preservation, ambition, idolatry, evil speaking, dissensions, until no space on his skin was left uncovered.

And I could see that on the tip of each arrow was a lethal poison and as soon as the arrow drove into his skin, he would spew forth poison and toxins from his lips by the bitter, critical words he spoke against those who opposed him or eventually those that he just plainly did not like or agree with.

And yet still he was ministering. In nation after nation and his movement was growing in nation after nation. For the Lord had kept His Word and had prospered him. But now, unlike the earlier years, money was flowing freely into the ministry.

And then the scene changed once again, this time into scenes of his home. He now had a beautiful home with every desire one could have wished for. And I saw his marriage and that behind closed doors he and his wife were like strangers. But still they taught others on marriage, and yet at home lived in two separate worlds.

And the entire chamber watched as his darling wife grew hard and brittle from lack of love and lack of care. And then I saw his wife, who had had the softest, most gentle of hearts toward Jesus – she who had been a worshipper and intercessor – as a woman spurned by her husband – excluded from the ministry – her heart grew cold in despair. And she became hedonistic, thinking only of materialism rather than the Lord.

The Lord bowed His head.

"Her heart was broken. If she had only come to Me and prayed, I could have changed all things. But she allowed her heart to become cold to My work and to My people and finally to My voice, until she who used to love communing with Me, shut Me out, even as she had been shut out by her husband.

"My child, there are those who sin, there are those who turn their backs on Me with full knowledge and awareness and will as to what they have done and what path they have chosen. Repentance is much harder for these. But there are also those who turn their backs on Me simply because their pain has become so overwhelming that the rejections and abandonments of others and their own heartbreak push them away from Me instead of towards Me. Tell My children, those who minister for Me, always to seek My face and ask My discernment so that I may show them MY heart.

"For many, many of these ones, who on the outside, look so hard to My gospel in their backsliding, are the very ones who yearn desperately to return to My love, but they feel if they did I would reject them. My child – these ones, whose hearts and motivations I well know, I will *never, never*, no, *never* cast out. Warn My children to weigh accurately – for there are still many, many who loved Me with fervor in their youth, who have through the harshness of life, rejected Me. But you see, child, I have not rejected them. And even as the hound of Heaven, I will continue to pursue them."

I saw Jesus look with a terrible sadness down on the man's wife.

"If just one Christian had loved her with a love that saw beyond her backslidden, cold ways, she could have returned to Me. But instead,

My child, they judged her in the prayer meetings, they judged her in the congregations, they judged her in the board meetings and she died prematurely in the hospital, hardly visited by him and unloved except by Me. For on her deathbed, she came to her senses. For there was one servant of Mine in the hospital who prayed.

"And before she died, tears streamed down her face in repentance and I came to her bedside and I held her hand fast in Mine. And how she shone, and the day before she died and crossed over to glory to be with Me, it was as though she had never been away."

Jesus closed his eyes. It was a holy moment.

And then a woman – a young woman – she was so beautiful, shining with the love and gentleness of God walked towards us. For some reason I knew she was wearing a pale blue robe. The man stared in horror, not daring to look up at Jesus. It was his wife.

So noble. Her eyes were radiant with the glory of God.

And without hesitation, she held out her hands to him.

He shook visibly and fell down before her, his face hidden in her robe. Her tears of joy fell on his hair. Slowly, ever so slowly, she knelt down opposite him and placed his face in her hands. Then gently – oh, so gently – she drew out the huge arrow, his side still bleeding. His entire right side had been gouged.

Jesus bent down and grasped her hand. How He loved this woman.

"There is no wound on Earth as terrible as a wound inflicted by a husband on a wife, or a wife on her husband. The marriage covenant is eternal."

Jesus turned to the man.

"By rejecting the wife of your youth, you gouged your own entire body in such a manner that it was almost impossible to recover."

He turned to me.

"My children who suffer the most are those who reject their spouse and then they themselves feel that they experience no pain. Divorce has become commonplace in My Body."

And Jesus drew in a deep, deep breath. I could see that this was causing Him the most intense, it seemed, terrible physical pain that made it almost impossible for Him to breathe. His voice became very soft.

"There are many, many of My children who walk at this time literally gouged and bleeding from the wounds of separation, divorce, and rejection. I long to heal them. Jezebel has been launched in full force against My Church in this present Church Age. Demon spirits of divorce and separation, of lust and lasciviousness. Battalions have been launched against My ministers. Many of My children are separating from their spouses and saying that it is condoned by Me. But, My child, know this. I have not condoned it."

Jesus turned to the man.

"You felt little pain as a result of rejecting your wife on Earth, and yet your wounds were even more desperate than your wife's. You were the one whose wounds were so desperate that they led to an early death."

Jesus nodded and at His instruction, the beautiful woman dressed in blue placed her hands onto the still-gaping wound. The wound instantly healed; his skin was like a newborn's.

And the man fell down before Jesus and cried desperately in repentance from the depths of his soul: "I am a sinner – Jesus, forgive me my sins! Forgive me my selfish ambition, my selfishness, my judgment."

And as he listed his sins, the tiny arrows clattered at once to the floor until just the one huge arrow that was speared in towards the left side of his heart remained.

The man turned to Jesus, questioning.

"When you were in your latter years, you began to realize the enormity of your fall from grace, but each time Our spirit overshadowed you – in dread of Our judgments – you pushed My presence away in dread."

Jesus looked with such compassion and love at the figure before Him.

"My son, arise." Jesus was quiet for a long moment.

"You believed there could never be redemption for you because you felt you had failed Me so terribly. You *did* fall from the faith, My son, but Our love and compassion for you is not equal to that of the way of Earth."

Jesus closed His eyes and with a fierce movement pulled out the final spear.

The man took a deep breath; then his entire countenance filled with an exquisite peace and an unfathomable joy flooded his countenance.

Jesus then laid His hand on the gaping wound which immediately healed, then brought the man's head to His breast. He smiled with radiant joy and tenderness.

"The Father's love. The joy of Heaven."

THE WOMAN EVANGELIST

I turned once again to the scenes playing out in front of me, and drew back, momentarily taken off guard. For somehow, immediately, I knew instinctively that this striking young woman on the screen was a well-known woman evangelist who had been a major visionary and evangelist in her generation.

I watched as the scenes of her childhood and early life passed in front of our eyes – then her second marriage and its subsequent demise. The vision slowed down to scenes of her early crusades in tents. I stared, captivated, watching her talking to the Father behind the stage.

No one else was there and somehow I could tell that this was such a sacred moment. Her face was rapt in love and adoration for the Father and Jesus, and she was crying out for His power and conviction to win souls. She was consumed with such a fervent passion for the lost that her tears fell onto the altar, as she pleaded with God for souls.

I turned to Jesus. I could see that, even watching this, He had been deeply moved.

"There are so many, many initiatives in today's ministry circles, My child, to equip My Church and prepare My believers. These are of utmost importance in the councils of Heaven and to My Father and Me.

"There are also specific churches and ministries in the Earth today to whom I have given a special commission to minister to My bride in her present state – to wash her, to cleanse her, to teach her and to prepare her for My coming. Many of these ministries are already walking in step with Me and, in the coming season, all who they have taught shall be part of My great and fearsome army to do battle for souls in the last days.

"But just as important in this next season is the urgency to win souls. I would have laid down My life for just one soul. Child, I would have shed My blood for just one soul, if that soul had come to know Me and once more be reconciled to My Father."

His eyes grew troubled.

"Many in My Church have lost their passion for SOULS. Many have lost their passion for soul-winning, yet when I walked on Earth, I came not for those who were whole, but for those in need of a physician. Many of My churches on the Earth today assemble with little thought for the lost.

"Their assemblies meet only their needs and not the needs of their neighbors, of their communities, of the lost and the dying around them.

"I died to save those who are lost. I laid down My life that this generation and all those that have gone before and are still to come may be saved from the clutches of hell and the evil one. It is *time for My children to take up My burden for the lost and go out.*

"Go out into the highways, go out in the byways. Proclaim My gospel to the lowly and unlovely and proclaim My gospel to the rich and the sinful."

The Lord looked at me with yearning.

"I *long* for My body to reach the lost."

I could see that the Lord was tremendously grieved that much of His Church did not seem to share His consuming passion for the lost and sinful.

"If My children will only preach My gospel, My Holy Spirit will bring in the harvest. The harvest is far greater today even than when I walked the Earth in My humanity, yet the laborers ..."

He stopped for a moment.

" ... The laborers are so few."

He turned back to the scene of the young woman evangelist weeping and pleading for souls at the altar. I watched as her ministry grew from the farms to a tent and a traveling revival. At first her husband was with her, but I saw as through the years the situation changed. And I saw Jesus watching with sorrow as private scenes played out, and through the years her marriage slowly fell apart until her husband left and they divorced.

Jesus turned and looked at me that look of intense love but intense knowing.

"My child, you are religious in your present thinking . . . ," He continued.

"There was so little teaching in her day, My child. She knew what My Word said, but My call and the Father's call upon her life burned so strongly that she was consumed with it. And she understood only a little of the principles of husband and wife in the ministry. My Church today has the privilege of so much teaching in the area of marriage and relationships and ministry. So many teachers trained by My Holy Spirit, so many resources, books, modern media.

"My daughter married more out of loneliness than out of My call, and in the following years greatly did she suffer for it. She had much less knowledge than My Church and ministers today."

He turned and looked me straight in the eye.

"She was less accountable than most in My Church today. And she was forgiven much."

I nodded in understanding, deeply moved by the Lord's compassion and understanding. I watched as she started a new phase of ministry; huge auditoriums were now being filled.

She stood in flowing robes on a great stage, her head flung back, preaching her heart out and thousands and thousands of unchurched people, thousands and thousands of sinners, came every night from the bars and the streets and the dens of iniquities up to the altar and committed their lives to Jesus Christ. Oh *how the sinners loved her*, for she was not religious, she just preached the Jesus who had forgiven the woman in adultery.

And the ministry grew strong and powerful, and she NEVER lost her focus for the lost. And I could sense that the Lord and the Father were greatly moved by passion for souls for their Kingdom.

Thousands came to the services every night, month after month, year after year. The Lord granted her favor even at the city gates. She evangelized, using the arts, and made the first forays into the media, directly challenging the prince of the power of the air.

But towards her latter days, I saw in the spirit realm a violent assignment rising up against her. And I saw the sign – RELIGIOUS DEVILS. These were nasty, heinous and vicious devils.

And I saw in the city in which she lived huge battalions of these devils unleashed on the work of God under her care. And where she had been previously courted by the media, she was now labeled a sensationalist and attention seeking by the religious sector and the media and many of her methods were scoffed at.

At first she was steadfast and courageous in her soul, facing the many persecutions, but then I saw her crumpled and alone, again at the altar.

The Lord had sorrow in His eyes.

"There became few that she could trust, so few that she could trust with knowing the intimate struggles of her own soul. Even those among her immediate family sought to control her decisions and her ministry. The Jezebelic spirit assigned against her ministry in the latter years began to isolate her and make her mistrusting of almost all.

"There were also many wounds by those who had professed friendship, some by those who had professed deep friendship. Some by close family. Those wounds were the hardest. And to protect herself, she began to close off her heart. There were many acquaintances. My child, many who surrounded her for the power and sway and the influence of the ministry, but none she could bare her soul to.

"She would come to Me many nights and weep before Me.

"Beloved, tell My children, especially My ministers, that those who hate you hated Me first. Those who wound you wounded Me first. Wounds are sure to come. Betrayers are sure to betray, even as I was betrayed. But it is not a reason to close off one's heart from the good and the pure and the lovely.

"The greatest steward of every wife's heart, My Father, ordained to be her husband, and the greatest steward of each husband's heart, his wife. The devil has attacked this union violently in this present generation. But I made them one, one in heart, one in flesh, that they might comfort one another, counsel one another and because their lives are laid down for one another, counteract the attacks of the enemy.

"There are many today whose marriages are under assault and many who stand alone. But, My child, for every life, I have surrounded My children with those who are directly from My hand, who are entrusted to be true stewards of My heart and of their hearts.

"Tell My suffering children that even in the wounds they suffer at this present time, there are those from My hand who will not wound them. They need not shut their hearts to these, for in these ones I have placed My healing balm. And in the darkest nights of the soul, these are My treasures that I place with each life. These ones are handpicked by Me to stand in MY place to love their hearts on Earth as I would love them.

"The devil would especially seek to isolate My ministers from these Aarons, from these armor-bearers, through the wounds of ministry. Some of these Aarons are old and trusted friends from decades past, others are those I have brought into their lives more recently. But each

I have chosen is directly from My hand and carries My heart. If My children ask for discernment, discernment I will give them on whom to entrust their heart.

"I will reveal who holds My heart – and theirs. Many of My ministers today struggle with agonizing sin and agonies of their souls, because they trust in no man and, therefore, have no man to turn to."

I watched as the evangelist was flung on the floor, unseen by the crowds, unseen by the staff, beset by persecutions and lies, assigned by Jezebel and religious spirits, crying out at the altar, but so isolated that even those who knew her pain no longer had access to her.

For she allowed no access, for she trusted no one.

I watched, in shock as the Lord gently raised His hand, and I could see the wounds from religious spirits. There were hundreds of bright red, still bleeding, small but vicious cuts all across her body. None were healing, but then I saw, that as two began to heal, they were slashed open again by religious devils from another source. Then I saw huge welts and bruises that were green and purple across her shoulders and back as though she had literally been lashed violently by a whip.

"Jezebel," I cried, knowing the sting of that evil and intimidating spirit. "Oh, Jesus, what do we do, we who minister for You, for the wounds and persecutions come?"

Jesus moved towards me and gently took my hand.

"To those who are married, beloved, guard that sacred union with all your heart. For you are each a steward of the other's heart and great protection I have provided in that union. Each wound you bear, when shared and ministered to, will heal more swiftly."

And I saw a wife weeping, devastated, and I saw a great, gaping wound in her heart. Her husband placed his arms around her and prayed for her.

And instantly, *instantly*, the wound healed and disappeared.

The Lord smiled knowingly.

"The devil has sought to place a divide between a man and the woman. That is why the enemy of your soul will always fight a woman's need for intimacy and a man's reluctance to give it."

Jesus smiled in understanding. Oh, how He knew His sons and daughters.

"But My men improve with age," He added with his great humor. And He looked at me knowingly.

"And My women become wiser. . . ."

We laughed, for I knew He wasn't letting me off the hook!

"But, My child, I have also given friends after My own heart. When a true friend prays, beloved, when a friend I have sent from Heaven prays, My healing balm will heal *all* wounds for love covers *all.*"

My eyes fell back onto the evangelist's purpled, bruised, covered shoulders.

"Was there no one?" I whispered.

"Her children loved her with a great and powerful love, and often in the early years, it was their love that healed many of her early wounds, for *how* she loved them also."

And then I saw a third marriage and I could see that, at this marriage, the Lord was *very* disturbed.

"But, Lord, she walks with You, she ministers still powerfully for You, and she hears Your voice."

The Lord looked at me again with infinite compassion.

"She was Our great treasure," He said softly.

"Loneliness on Earth, My child, is a terrifying thing for those who suffer and carry great wounds. Even for My ministers, sometimes especially for My ministers. My Father created mankind for fellowship and the human soul cries out for that fellowship, fellowship with US and fellowship with others of My children. The more wounded a servant of mine becomes, the more his or her discernment and judgment of situations will become clouded. And eventually, her loneliness and need for companionship overrode her discernment, and My still, small voice, and she married a man who used her and the ministry."

"Which only increased her pain," I whispered.

Jesus nodded.

I watched as through her shortly lived, third marriage she still preached with passion, her inner pain covered so well that few knew the anguish she suffered. The scenes moved on to the latter part of her life and I saw her lying in bed. Still, she talked to the Lord, for her only joy. He was her only rest. He was, even in her frailty and human weaknesses, her only treasure apart from her children, on Earth and beyond. She was studying a sermon she had yet to preach and reached out and opened a bottle of sleeping pills.

I watched as her body was discovered the next morning. No one would ever know the true circumstances of her death, but her works live on today. And her powerful stance for evangelism still stands and generations have been touched and impacted by her life and by her ministry. And still are.

Suddenly, I felt the strong presence of the Lord suddenly over-shadow me. I knew if I should dare look up, what I would find. Eventually, I raised my head.

There, standing in front of me, clinging to Jesus, leaning on Him, looking to His every word, was the woman evangelist. The light surrounding her was blinding in its purity and magnificence.

Her hair fell past her shoulders and her face was unlined, her skin was beautiful and she was free from *all* care. There were no wounds or bruises, her skin was milk-white without blemish. From her exuded the presence of God, the glory of God, the tender compassions of God. She looked at me and began to speak.

"I was called as a visionary. And as a visionary, I lived and pioneered in a time before the Church received understanding of women evangelists in ministry and before many understood evangelism using the media. I suffered great misunderstandings and wounds for it. If I had not isolated myself because of previous wounds, I would have found healing and I would have been saved from many, many unwise decisions . . . ."

She looked upon me tenderly.

"More in my personal life than in the ministry," she continued.

"You, and many like you, have been called to see beyond, to see and describe what to many still remains behind a veil. Misunderstandings will come, child," she said gently and took my hand.

I could feel the incredible love and compassion flowing from her to me. She drew me to her and, as she drew me, I felt a release of pain – the pain of standing for so many, many years fighting in the media, fighting for the airwaves, fighting for all the evangelistic media projects that lay ahead, which were yet to come upon the Earth.

"I have known you because of your call to media. My call was to be an evangelist, but I was called to evangelize through the beginnings of media as it was in my day. Through the arts and drama, and then eventually radio."

She held me away from her and smiled as a mother to a child.

"And now there is television," she said softly in wonder, "and coming soon so much, much more."

She took my arm and walked with me. Jesus watched us both walking as His daughters, as sisters.

"Apostles, prophets and evangelists to the media will in this next season become commonplace, but for you like me, it is not in this present Church Age greatly understood. You and others like you will make it plain so that the next generation will see more clearly and run faster and do more exploits. Things are about to change. You are part of this change."

I watched as she held up a huge crystal vial filled with what somehow I knew to be her very own tears that she had cried on Earth. She took my hand gently.

"Because each tear that you and those who are called like you shed, each tear shed from misunderstanding and the loneliness of standing for what is not yet commonplace, is captured in a vial by My Father."

"You are the Father's treasure. In your latter years you will encourage His media army greatly. You will teach them to fight and be courageous and never give up in the face of the fiercest onslaught of the devil. Many others will teach also. You and your husband have carried a call to media in this generation. This coming young generation have been baptized into a call to media. They will take great courage from your exploits and the exploits of others. They will take great fortitude from what you have already accomplished and from what lies ahead. For what lies ahead in media for you is so much greater than even what you have seen. Even the projects that have been ordained for you are coming quickly and will open an apostolic gate to media in the arena of entertainment and generations of Satan's strongholds in this arena will be shattered even in an instant. And through these gates the next generation will march. An entire generation will be impacted in this next season of media evangelism."

Once again she drew me to herself.

"Be faithful," she said softly. "Keep your eyes on the lover of your soul. And your Heavenly Father."

And she walked off towards a man who took her hands in his and embraced her.

The Lord looked after them both tenderly.

"Her first husband . . . ," I uttered in wonder, knowing he had died when they were on the mission field so many, many years before.

"Yes," said the Lord. "They were reunited when she crossed over into glory coming to be with Us."

Jesus closed His eyes.

"There are many who will read these words that are of the next generation, many who were born into My Kingdom for such a time as this, in the times of the end. A great baptism of the media has been released upon the young generation at this present time – they will do great exploits in the media, they will turn tables on the devil and even as I turned over the tables in My Father's temple, they will turn over the tables of the devil's grip and stronghold on the media – I am raising up in this and in the generation to follow filmmakers and screenwriters and artists, musicians and directors and producers and writers and documentary makers who will literally shatter the strongholds of the spirit of Babylon and Jezebel with which the devil has sought to ensnare and entrap this last generation through the entertainment industry – it will be demolished because those laborers I have called to the media are RISING."

THE UNLOVELY

*J*esus looked out over the assembly in the Throne Room.

"Beloved child – My Church enters a season where times will become dark, much darker than in previous Church ages, even to the time of My disciples when they were persecuted so relentlessly. Tell My children that they enter into the season of the beginning of sorrows before the end of all things as they have previously known them." He stopped with a terrible sorrow in His eyes. "And they are unprepared."

"Battalions are preparing to be launched; violent assignments are being launched as we speak to hinder My work and the work of My servants to proclaim My gospel. In the present world you live in, it is almost unthinkable to be put in prison for My sake, but My child, there yet comes a day . . . ."

"It is essential that My children drink from Me, get their source of encouragement from Me, or they will not stand in the days ahead. For in the days ahead, every work they do for Me, if it is a true work, shall be greatly opposed on all sides, both by wicked men and by wicked spirits unleashed against My true servants. All those who stand the test of fortitude, endurance and perseverance will prevail, but those who depend on their sustenance and encouragement from others will shrivel and grow weary and faint. Tell My children to come and draw from the true vine, come and drink from the living waters from My hand. For truly I tell you that it is only those who hear My voice and follow My leading in the outpouring of sorrows who shall truly prevail. Endurance. Fortitude."

He said again, "No cheap grace. Grace is never cheap. Grace

demanded My life, My heart. Grace demanded My all. It demands no less of you, My child. It demands no less of the least of My followers. Take up your cross each day, whether it be standing when all is dark and encouragement is far from you. When everything within you screams, give up, give in. Stand fast on what you know; stand fast in what I have commissioned you to do. Stand fast against the wiles of the evil one, stand fast against the stout words and persecutions of wicked men and stand fast against the agonizing arrows of those who are not wicked but are deceived and who persecute you. And turn the other cheek. Bless them. Love them. Pray for them."

He looked at me, His eyes boring into my soul. And I saw the glimmering of a smile on his lips. 'Fervently . . . ,' He added. "For they know not what they do.

"Love – My love casts out all fear, My child. You need not fear your enemies if you hold onto the law of love. Standing fast in the law of love confounds the prince of darkness, it puts to flight powers and principalities, it confuses and terrorizes wicked men and confounds deceived men. Walk in the Royal Law of Love. Lay down your life. Hold fast to what is good and true and lovely. For in the future, good and pure and lovely will be far from the grasp, save for those who keep it in their hearts. Obey My commands. Love My Father first and foremost with all your heart and your soul. Love My Father with all your mind. And love your neighbor as you love yourself.

"Tell My children that each time the enemy assails them, and they are bound with discouragement and doubt and lose the will to go on, that when they rise up and continue – that is endurance. That is fortitude. Tell My children that this holds great esteem in My sight. It is an easy thing to fight against an easily overpowered enemy. But to fight against true darkness of the soul, that is courage indeed."

A small, scrawny child appeared on the screen.

The Lord beckoned me closer.

The child was huddled in a corner, her dress was torn and her arms were tightly wrapped around her body, whimpering, whimpering.

"She was abused by her father when he was drunk, and she was beaten by her mother."

The scene sped up to when she was around sixteen and now an addict, needle marks all over her still scrawny arms. And she was pregnant.

And then I watched her standing outside the gates of a huge crusade, whether it was Billy Graham or another I do not know, but it was an evangelist preaching the Gospel of Jesus Christ in the center of a large city and her friends were jeering and at first she too jeered, but then the music came ringing out of the arena, and a tear fell down her face. And she looked around in amazement, as did her friends.

"But she had had a praying grandmother. And ever since she was five, she had been fascinated with a picture of Me on her grandmother's bedroom dresser. And when no one saw, she knelt down before My picture and said, 'Jesus, if you are real, come into my heart.'

"Shortly after that her grandmother died and she grew up beaten and abused, but I had never forsaken her. *And I had never forgotten her heartfelt prayer.*

"And My Holy Spirit drew her into the arena and she left her friends and stood with the crowd. And when the altar call was given, she walked up with hundreds of others and committed her life to Me.

"But she went back home with her friends and there was no one to disciple her or show her the way, and soon she was living in one room, with a baby on the way, with no father.

"And she slept with any man who would give her money to pay for her drug habit.

"The baby was born. A boy.

"But even though she was so far from Me or from fellowship with My children, in her pain and desperation, she held up her son and dedicated him to Me and begged Me to use him for My gospel."

The scene changed and I watched as the baby screamed and she got up to shake the babe, but then fell to her knees, crying out to Jesus – "Jesus, *help* me!"

And I saw her weeping over the bottles of gin and Jesus gently placed His hand onto my arm.

He put His finger to His lips.

I watched as she emptied the bottles down the toilet, picked up the screaming babe and placed him in the cot, then closed the door and ran, ran to her bedroom, flinging herself onto her bed sobbing, sobbing as though her heart would literally break, crying out for Jesus.

She took out a tattered Bible and sat sobbing, heartbroken, on the bed.

And then I saw Jesus standing next to her, soothing her brow just as one would with a much-beloved child.

"There, there," He soothed. And she calmed, as though she could sense His presence. Gradually, her sobbing stopped and she fell into a deep, deep peace-filled sleep.

The Lord looked at me long and hard. Then I saw an angel walk in and gently wake her. She awoke and looked at the phone and phone book next to her bed. And I saw the angel open the phone book to a ministry in her area for the unlovely, and her attention was drawn to it and she picked up the phone and dialed.

"My mainstream church still rejected her for many years until she was considered respectable enough to conform to their standards."

"But I never rejected her, My child."

"And My *true* ministers loved her and cared for her, and discipled her until she was strong enough to walk on her own. But she loved

Me with all her heart and pressed to her very limit and far beyond, she clung to Me and cried out for My aid, and My father and I took her up even as a babe in arms."

He turned again to the scenes of her life.

Years had passed and she was now old, with silver hair.

I stared amazed.

For now she was sitting with her husband in the front row of a huge auditorium with a congregation of what must have been 20,000.

And on the platform stood a fine young man.

Tall and handsome, dressed in a beautifully tailored suit.

He was the pastor of the congregation.

And I saw that it was Mother's Day. And he was talking to the congregation about his mother and then he asked her to rise and I saw her stand.

For it was *her* son, that babe in arms, born in squalor, dedicated to Jesus for His service.

Each day she got up.

Each day she confronted the demons from his past. And slowly taking ground by ground, she conquered them.

"Because she had such courage, when demons fought for her at every turn, still she cried out for Me. And because of her endurance and fortitude in the darkest period of her life, thousands of the unlovely are nurtured today.

"She is a mother to unwed mothers, a mother to the unlovely. And, what joy there was as she stood. For how loved and adored she was.

"And in that congregation were soup kitchens and outreaches to the homeless, and unwed mothers were welcome and addicts were commonplace."

"And there was *always* help for the needy."

"And no one, not one, was turned away."
Jesus turned to me, tears in His eyes.
"Truly – this is love."

THE PROPHET

I bowed my head, deeply moved by the scenes that had just played out before me. Oh, how infinite was the Lord's redemption.

Then, all at once, I sensed a great stillness as a holy, *holy* presence descended and I turned to see Jesus standing next to His Father's throne.

But it was the form of a man standing with Jesus that caught my attention. And this man seemed to be leaning his entire weight on the Lord.

I frowned. Something about the form seemed strangely familiar, and slowly the brilliance of the glory descending over them lifted slightly, but still I could not distinguish the man's features. But one thing I was certain of, this man who leaned on the Lord for his very sustenance was utterly devoted to Jesus Christ and exuded a fervency of love for Jesus that made me want to fall on my knees and weep.

And somehow I knew that this man was greatly adored by the Lord and highly esteemed. But, the greatest thing that struck me was the fervency of affection between them. And I saw the Lord tenderly stroke this man's head.

Then, instantly, Heaven receded, and Jesus stood next to me.

"Who is he, Lord?" I asked.

"He was one of the foremost prophets of your generation and the generations before. He operated in one of the most accurate and powerful prophetic and seer gifts ever bestowed upon a man by My Father's own hand."

The Lord closed His eyes, and a terrible sorrow crossed His

countenance. He sighed deeply. Oh, there was agonizing pain in His sigh. And I realized how deeply Jesus is moved by you and me still on Earth.

"He fell to major besetting sins in the latter days of his life. There was much controversy in much of My Church concerning both his repentance and the restoration process that followed."

The Lord continued.

"Violent assignments are presently being released against those I have raised up as prophets and seers at this present time. For it is Jezebel, their main opponent, who has been released – the great intimidator and tormentor of their souls.

"Tell My prophets, tell My seers, that it is time to set their faces as flint. It is time to set their faces to the battle. My order to march has gone out. In all the tumult and fierce battle that they walk through, it is imperative that they look only to Me.

"Many will be the clamors for their attention.

"Many will be the baptisms of rejection and misunderstandings.

"Many will suffer because they refuse to march to the voice of man, but in these end days they MUST march only to My voice."

The Lord's voice was strong. Commanding, and yet with such mercy.

He sighed. "The prophet is one who hears My voice. The seer sees that which is only visible and audible in the spirit realm. The enemy knows full well that if he can hinder My servants' seeing and hearing, many of the most vital and strategic instructions and warnings from Heaven in this last dispensation of the Church will be lost, will go unrecorded and, therefore, unheeded.

"Millions in My present army in this generation will suffer for this.

"Millions who could have been saved from destruction will not hear the timings and the strategies of Heaven.

"*That* is why Jezebel has assigned those who hear and see with such violence in this present season.

"And it was Jezebel who assigned this."

Heaven receded and I saw a heavily pregnant woman, a bondservant of the Lord, in travail in the spirit. And I saw an angel stand before her and proclaim: "Your prayers have risen up to the throne of God. This child shall be My bondservant who will preach the gospel to many, many in the end days. For the Lord God of Hosts has heard your prayer."

And I saw this baby being born, a boy.

And I saw the angels at his birth surrounding him and his mother. And there was great rejoicing in Heaven. And I heard the sound of a trumpet and the proclamation.

"For he shall proclaim My Word to the ends of the Earth. And in the wind and in the fire his words shall come.

"For, he shall speak that which he hears from the throne and he shall speak that which he sees in the heavenly realms. And many, many, many will come to My light and come to the knowledge of My Son because of the words of wind and the words of fire."

And I saw the most exquisitely carved golden box, and in this box was a gift, and the box came directly from the hand of the Father and was given to the Son. And when Jesus opened the lid, the blazing white incense of Heaven filled the room in which the babe was born.

And I watched as Jesus removed a small rock, covered with moss and earth from the box that looked like the peat of Scotland.

And as the Lord turned the rock within His hand, it started to blaze. With rubies – which I sensed were the words of the prophet, then with sapphires. The sapphires, I sensed, were the seer realm and then with diamonds, which were words that would only be released in the latter, latter days. I sensed that each diamond was a word that would bring the Church into a higher level according to the revelation of God's plans revealed from Heaven for the end times.

Then the Lord took the stone and placed it directly into the babe's heart.

The Father's gift.

And I knew that this gift would be forged in pain in this infant's life.

That the rubies, sapphires and diamonds, intermingled with the rock and the peat and the moss, that he would remember always the source of the gift. That the gift giver would always be foremost in his heart.

And I saw the Lord smile upon his mother, for she was also much beloved by Him.

And then I saw this prophet as a youth, and I saw the Lord Jesus often walking next to him, often in conversation. And it was the Lord's joy to be with His prophet. And it was the sapling prophet's joy to be with his Master.

And as the years went by, I saw his steps directed in a very, very specific way by the angelic host. And he was mentored by one who also saw and was a seer. For the Lord had commissioned it. And it had been ordained by Heaven.

And the gift grew in strength, and the gift was hewn from the rock in the form of exquisitely polished rubies, and blazing sapphires that shone with clarity and the blues of the angelic and heavenly visions that were given to him. And he moved in humility and power and in accuracy. And many, many lives were saved from destruction because of his obedience to the Lord.

But then I saw several times throughout his life times of darkness, and spirits assailing him. And he would retreat from the public eye for a season, but the Lord would bring him out by His own hand.

And in the latter days of his life, he ministered in magnificence for the gift flowed in fullness in accuracy and in power and he was received by many in diverse denominations and movements and in the high places of the Earth. And I saw him standing on a platform, the Lord looking on with great joy, and I saw that as he delivered the Word of the Lord, huge and perfectly carved diamonds from the rock jettisoned out, not only to that arena but all across the Earth in the spirit realm and, it was as if the angelic host had been waiting for its declaration on Earth and, the angelic shofars blew. And I saw Heaven's battalions marching, and I knew the Lord had entrusted him with a mighty power from on High to move Heaven and the realms of the damned.

But then, in the latter days of his life, I saw, as a great cloud of darkness arose on the horizon against the Church, I saw a great blackened mist rising.

And then I distinguished that there were forms in the mist, thousands of battalions of evil, demonic forms and they held a banner high that read – 'WAR AGAINST THE SAINTS.'

And the banner was dipped in blood and the blood was still fresh and dripping from the banner.

And the demonic princes were exhilarated by the blood and I knew that their greatest exultation was in causing great pain of the minds, bodies and souls of the saints.

And these battalions were marching, demonically energized, as to their mission against the saints that lay ahead.

And then, the king of the central battalion rode around to the front and held up a huge, black, iron, gleaming sword and behind flew a second banner that read in jagged black script – 'JEZEBEL.'

And I knew that this was their first act of massacre in the spirit realm. They had been commissioned by hell to discredit and malign and intimidate the prophets and seers of God, and then to throw a net to entice them into the entanglements of sin or sickness.

And I saw the prophet isolated and alone in his chamber, huddled over certain reading materials, and I saw him struggle for breath and throw down the papers in powerlessness and despair. And on these papers were written criticisms about him and his ministry.

Mistruths, lies and half truths. And I saw him study these week after week and grow despondent and weary. And I saw a cockatrice rising off the critical words of deceived men, and I saw an unprotected portion of his soul, and the cockatrice found entrance and nested there. And it seemed it was in hibernation, quite comfortable and hidden from view.

The years went by, and I saw the prophet once again in his chamber, struggling with his health. Although greatly loved, he was now isolated and I watched as he pored over a computer, agonizing again at certain lies and mistruths that were being propagated about both him and his ministry.

And I watched as the hidden cockatrice in the prophet's heart began to move and each criticism and each wound seemed to issue thousands of flies who demonically attached themselves to the prophet and found their way to where the cockatrice had lain dormant for years. And the cockatrice began to lay her eggs – thousands and thousands and thousands of eggs. And the flies laid another source of eggs. I watched as the eggs even became a film over the prophet's eyes and over his soul.

The Lord watched with me.

"He became wounded by other's opinions of himself and his ministry and started to defend his position on many things," the Lord said softly.

"Instead of forgiving his enemies and trusting in Me to defend and vindicate him if I saw fit to do so, every criticism of his prophetic ministry became personal and caused festering wounds that in turn attracted demonic spirits toward his soul.

"His initial discouragement became self-pity. His self-pity became a deep mire of depression. His depression led him into despair and a driving need for comfort. He started to drown his sorrows in alcohol and then in fleeting homosexual acts, committing fleshly sins to gain fleeting comfort for his soul. He craved peace. He craved rest from torment. But the comfort and the peace from sin became so fleeting. Because he had, from his conception, such a tender and intimate relationship with Me, the conviction after he committed certain acts drove him even more intensely to despair, to desperation.

"Even to thoughts of suicide.

"And so the hidden cycle continued. And he became a master of deception and, in turn, a slave to Jezebel.

"As her slave, he manifested deceit and lies and his soul became veiled.

"He no longer walked in truth.

"But still the gift operated in great power, for the gift is given without repentance.

"But because he could no longer live in peace with himself or in peace with Me and My Father, he needed to escape again, and so he committed more sin, to escape the conviction of My Holy Spirit.

"Finally, he lived continually in that most tormented of places – a dark, dark night of his soul. Loving Me, wanting to serve Me, crying out fervently to Me in the torment of his night-time hours, yet on waking, he was driven to sin again until sin became so entrenched in his flesh that it became besetting sin and became a lifestyle.

"The deceived became the deceiver.

"Eventually he deceived and lied to everyone . . . except to Me."

"Oh, Lord," I cried, for I felt such mercy and compassion emanating from the Lord, yet His face was set and I sensed His judgment.

"The primary assignment against him was his mind. The primary assignment against My prophets, against My seers is against their minds." Jesus was quiet for a moment.

"Lying, slandering, divisive battalions of the enemy have been unleashed in great measure at this present time to tear down My servant's credibility, with one aim – that their works – that which they see and that which they hear from above, may be discredited and maligned.

"When My servants that minister for Me in this day and in this hour, move from the safety and security of My Father's protection in the secret place to defend themselves and their ministries, they become a target to be violently assailed by the spirit of Jezebel. Her power to malign, and her power to slander grows the fastest when it is fed. It is fueled sometimes by wicked men but mostly by unenlightened, deceived men who fuel her spirit by their own propagation and circulation of her false reports.

"Even though it is sometimes greatly testing for my servants when they and their ministries are lied about and criticized, but if they keep their eyes on Me, Jezebel will hold no power over them."

I knew that what the Lord was about to say was terribly important and a key for all of us in present ministry and all who would soon follow, when my own children would react to her intimidations.

"If, when criticized, My servant had given every wound and every persecution truly to Me, discouragement could not have assailed his soul in the overwhelming manner that you saw.

"If My servant had viewed the great ministry gift he carried as MY ministry, not as his, he would not have had to fight in his heart so vehemently against mistruths and lies.

"He would have understood that it is MY battle, not his.

"If he had kept his eyes only on Me, I would have been the source of his comfort, his joy and his peace, and no besetting sin could have taken hold of him."

The Lord smiled sadly.

"I do not condemn My servants when through their own set of frailties, they fall, IF they *truly repent* and ask for restoration, My Father and I will freely forgive them and restore them. Above all things, keep yourselves from idolatry.

"My servant lost precious time on Earth, and his calling was greatly hindered. The devil well knew this. And it was his strategy to weaken his witness in the end times, when it was to have the greatest impact."

He looked at me, His eyes flashed with fire.

"My child, live only for what is spoken about you in Heaven.

"Care nothing for what is spoken or written on Earth that does not find its foundation in Me.

"Care only about the reputation you hold with Myself and My Father.

"Care nothing for any reputation that you may hold on Earth, no matter how noble, nor how slanderous.

"People's view of you will change from hour to hour. Many are My servants who have lived in ministry in continual torment, enslaved to others opinion of their works and of themselves.

"Jezebel's greatest enemy – her greatest terror – comes from those of My servants who through great sufferings and death to their own reputation and own ambitions have learned to ignore her continual calls to war and hostility.

"From My servants who, even when their reputation and calling is violently attacked, choose to ignore her intimidations and abide continually in the shadow of My Father's presence.

"This renders her completely helpless.

"She greatly fears these ones and cowers at their presence.

"Care only for My opinion, child."

He started to walk up the nave.

"And truly you will know peace."

Jesus disappeared and once again I saw Him at the throne, with the prophet who was so greatly beloved by Him and His Father still leaning on Him, now with his head on His breast.

And as the glory softened, I recognized the face of the man.

I had always loved him. His self-deprecating humor, his mercy, his humility, his love for the next generation, caused many, many of us in the following generation to love and honor him.

He had been, indeed, greatly loved.

And he had, indeed, greatly fallen.

I watched as he walked down the nave, clutching the Lord, his head still resting on Jesus' breast, his tears falling onto Jesus' hands.

And Jesus stroked his hands, continually stroked his hands.

Oh, how restored and how forgiven he was here in eternity.

For now he walked with the One who was comfort, who was rest, who was peace. And tears fell down his cheeks over the Lord's hands and Jesus wept too.

And it was such a holy, sacred moment that passed between them that I bowed my head.

But I sensed that there were still diamonds that were yet unspoken by this man that would be of great importance to the Church in the days ahead.

And I knew that the Lord had wanted me to see Him with him.

"You have come a long way, beloved."

Jesus looked at me with great love, the man's head still resting on His breast.

"So have many like you. Pray for those who persecute you. Bless those who despitefully use you. And you will all go still further . . . ."

And the caution came.

" . . . if you keep your eyes on Me."

THE MISSIONARIES

*J*esus and the prophet of God disappeared and I watched as the brilliance of Heaven receded and I felt that finally the unveiling was complete.

But then I heard the sound of singing and I was taken into a plain room.

It was a church of some sort, and there were six or seven oriental-looking women singing along with one man. Their voices were discordant and even shrill, but their faces beamed and they sang in Cantonese or Mandarin, I know not which. An elderly woman led the singing, and finally an elderly man rose up and preached to the tiny congregation in their own language.

I watched as the church service ended, and the congregation plied the old couple with simple gifts and embraced them fervently.

And then I saw the couple in one bare and simple room, packing two huge steamer trunks. The man seemed very weak. He sat on the edge of the bed and his wife handed him a cup of water. He had a coughing paroxysm and the tears streamed down his cheeks. They held each other, both were weeping.

I heard the Lord's voice from behind me.

"They were called as missionaries to China when they were both in their youth. They left the shores of America immediately after their wedding. They were eighteen and nineteen respectively."

I watched as the old woman picked up a wedding photograph. They were both strikingly handsome in the photo. She had long, gleaming, dark, hair, and he was tall and the epitome of the 'all-American' young evangelist. I sensed it was the 1920s. I watched as they left New York

Harbor with the same two steamer trunks, exhilarated with the Lord's vision to reach China with His gospel. After weeks on the sea they arrived.

The Lord continued.

"It was not as they had expected. The mission board was run at that time by those with conservative and religious views and they were considered too inexperienced to minister to the people. And his preaching was considered too radical. They were not welcomed. For the first five years, she cleaned the mission house and served while he tended the gardens. Their dreams of radically touching China with My gospel faded."

The Lord smiled.

"But we heard his cries and I sent one of My faithful servants to their city. He was an old British missionary and he embraced them and fathered them. Soon they learned Cantonese and Mandarin and the young missionary traveled everywhere My older servant went.

"Each night, the three would sit together and pray for China to open up to My gospel."

Jesus turned to the throne, and I saw their prayers rising as burning incense before the Father's throne. Heaven was intent on each prayer and then I saw the Father commissioning hosts of angels. And the angels took the incense of the prayers and I saw them dispatched to Earth to move on the hearts of both the unsaved and consecrated men to open doors for the gospel.

Then I saw a great flurry of excitement and I saw, as the small and insignificant group huddled over candlelight, how they started to translate the Bible into different languages. I watched as they poured out their lives, ministering to small groups of people in the daytime and praying and translating at night. This went on for years.

Finally, the English missionary became very old and was called back to England.

He took the younger's hand with his own frail one.

"Be faithful," he rasped. "Fulfill the work of the Lord. Live only for Him."

And they embraced. They never saw him again on Earth.

The couple continued, year after year, faithfully ministering, praying and translating, until they were in their late seventies when the husband became sick, needing treatment in America.

I watched as they boarded the ship that was to take them to America. All of their worldly possessions were in those same two steamer trunks.

And in the cabin, I saw the man putting his hand upon the woman's shoulder as she sobbed in anguish. And she sobbed night after night and was inconsolable.

"She cries for China?" I whispered.

The Lord smiled with such mercy and such compassion. He looked at me tenderly.

"Yes, she cries for China, beloved." His voice was very soft. "But she cries also for all their youthful dreams deferred.

"For all the great crusades that were not to be, for all the thousands of souls to be saved when there were few decisions for My gospel made.

"She cries for all the days and nights – the years of poured out lives – yet so little in the natural that she can see with her eyes.

"Her heart is broken.

"They gave everything to preach My gospel, beloved, but they have seen little fruit on Earth.

"They landed at the harbor with no one to meet them. They lived for the remainder of their days in a simple, rented tenement building in New York, still praying. There was one invitation to speak at a small church one Christmas and they dressed in their Christmas best.

"The church was small and uncared for. There were forty people inside, chewing gum and disinterested, apart from a few.

"The missionary spoke about China. About commitment to preach the Gospel of Jesus Christ and then opened up the altar. Only two people came to the front. One middle-aged lady and a fourteen-year-old boy. He prayed with them.

"Not long after, the old man died. There was no one at his funeral except the lady who loved him and he was buried in a simple coffin with a simple gravestone that read, 'Christ is my all.' She died a month later.

"And there was no more remembrance of them on Earth."

The Lord raised His hand and a blinding brilliance issued from behind Him.

He looked at me long and hard.

"They were obedient," He said. "They were obedient to My voice."

He turned.

Behind Him stood the couple, radiant. Glorious in the brilliance that emanated from them.

He looked around forty; she looked as if she was in her late thirties. They were young and strong and glowing with joy and life.

I literally felt streams of abundant LIFE flowing from their very beings.

She was dressed in the most beautiful of robes, intricately embroidered with pearls, and they both wore capes trimmed with ermine as royals do on Earth.

They knelt before their throne as the book was opened.

I heard the voice of the Father in power, authority and might say, "RISE, esteemed son and daughter of the King."

And, as they rose up, the assembly in the Throne Room transformed.

An angel blew a shofar and proclaimed: "The prayers of the son and daughter of the great King."

And an angel brought a great vial to the throne.

It seemed to be an enormous crystal jar, and inside was a burning white mist.

And at the Father's command, Jesus poured it out upon the altar before the throne. The white, burning mist hung over the altar, then moved like lightning to the four corners of the assembly which changed to a different chamber.

This was like one of Earth's modern-day stadiums, except it had no end.

And I saw millions and millions and millions of Chinese and oriental faces, stretching for what must have been hundreds of miles back.

I could not see the end of it.

Jesus turned to me, deeply moved.

"Their faithful, faith-filled prayers brought China to her knees. Their faithful prayers opened up doors of utterances on every level of the nation."

He walked closer to me and took my face in His hands.

"There are many things you and many others of My children have walked through, that because you have only seen through a glass darkly, you have become greatly discouraged at what your life has been poured out for and yet you have not yet seen the fruit of your labors."

He raised His hand.

And I saw the underground Church, worshipping the Father and Jesus in total adoration.

"They poured out their lives for Me, yet saw so little fruit on Earth.

"They received so little encouragement for their souls, except from Me.

"They received little if any affirmation from men.

"Their reputation was of no consequence to the sons and daughters of Earth. And their accomplishments went unseen.

"But, My child, this son and this daughter played a major unseen role in the rising of My Church in China. Because of their obedience to Me and My instructions throughout their ministry, their translations live in millions of homes today. Their faithful and unceasing prayers affected the entire nation and the spread of the gospel in this land. This, in turn, will affect the whole Earth in My next move with what lies ahead for China.

"Many, many of My children live in obscurity, their noble works for Me unseen by most and unappreciated by many. Many of My ministers' works are seen, but the persecutions that accompany them are deeply painful."

We turned to look back at the couple, radiant with fulfillment of the commission that the Father had placed in their hearts so many, many years before.

"There is one more thing," Jesus continued.

I watched as a young man preached to hundreds of thousands. There were no cameras, no media there, but his major ministry was to the unreached people groups. And thousands were coming to salvation every night.

I frowned. I did not see the connection.

"The fourteen-year-old boy who committed his life at the altar because of the old missionaries call?" the Lord spoke quietly. "His fruit also is credited to their account."

And I heard a trumpet blow. And I saw the radiant couple kneeling to receive their crowns.

The crown of a soul winner.

The crown of life.

And a great veil fell across the scene and the revelation ended.

And I knew that the Lord's compassion for all who would read this book, who had poured out their lives for Him on Earth, was indescribable.

That the Lord Jesus and the Father Himself knew every tear that was shed.

Every prayer that was said.

Every soul led to the Lord.

Every orphan loved and fed.

Every widow cared for.

Every heartfelt song sung.

Every book written.

Every sermon preached.

The sick healed.

The broken-hearted bound up.

Every family raised for His glory.

Every heartfelt struggle to preach the gospel in the face of immense opposition.

He knew every heart of courage, fortitude and perseverance to preach His gospel and the gospel of His beloved Son.

Even in the most barren of times . . .

All was seen by *Him*.

All was recorded by Him.

Every tear was collected.

All was treasured by Him.

And one day in eternity all would be revealed when the great veil is lifted.

And all that we see only darkly on Earth will be made clear.

In that most glorious of moments . . .

When we finally look upon His face . . . .

VOLUME FOUR

THE GREAT SIFTING BEFORE
THE RELEASE OF THE NEXT
GREAT AWAKENING

*T*he Throne Room disappeared.

Jesus held out His hand to me.

I grasped it tightly.

And instantly we were in another dimension.

Somehow, I knew that we were now standing in the Supreme Court of the kingdom of darkness.

I watched as Satan and his princes and his legal counsels were in deep, earnest consultation.

Satan had a look of vicarious triumph on his face.

Lying on a vast table before the councils were thousands – maybe tens of thousands – of what I instantly understood to be meticulously documented files.

And somehow, I knew that Satan's gloating was connected with every human soul that was represented by these same files.

I also knew that the men and women who were represented before the councils of hell were greatly hated.

And *greatly* feared by both Satan and his powers and principalities.

These men and women were causing hell and the kingdom of darkness great and terrible setbacks.

They were literally plundering the kingdom of darkness by their prophetic intercession, by their apostolic and prophetic mandates and by their powerful end-time evangelistic and marketplace anointing.

They had been anointed and appointed to seize previously uncharted territory of the enemy.

And take it by force.

The enemy had suffered greatly for this.

There had started to be many losses among the principalities and powers in the areas of finance. Government. The family. The Entertainment Industry.

The satanic princes and powers that had held these territories had started to suffer heavy setbacks.

But there was an even greater threat against Satan's kingdom rising on the horizon.

The advent of the greatest end-time outpouring of the Father's mantle of glory that the Earth had ever known.

An outpouring that would literally *tear* down the strongholds of the enemy.

An outpouring of the greatest glory, the greatest awakening, the greatest wave. A literal tsunami of healings and creative miracles.

An outpouring of the Father's holiness.

An outpouring of the Father's grace.

An outpouring of the Father's great and manifold compassions.

The outpouring of the FATHER'S LOVE.

And *each* of the books that lay before Satan's councils represented a man or a woman – a boy or a girl, whose lives were specifically mandated to usher in and to release this next move of Almighty God.

And the kingdom of hell was now about to strike back in desperation.

In violence and cruel assault against God's end-time champions.

The cry went up from Satan's courts.

"We go to the High Courts of Heaven – we sue for their souls!"

The scene changed and we were sitting in what appeared to be an enormous courtroom in the third heaven.

Very like the courtrooms of Earth and yet it was different.

Thousands of files were stacked to the ceilings.

The files of the righteous.

I saw as the accuser, the serpent, the devil himself, plus his legions of legal scribes entered the court rooms of Heaven.

I watched as book after book of life was opened.

And I heard the very words I had read in Job,

"Take away the hedge . . . take away the hedge."

Suddenly it seemed that a thousand courtrooms opened up.

And the cry of the accuser resounded from every one.

"Take away the hedge. And they shall curse you."

And I sensed the immense suffering of the Great Judge, the Father.

And a terrible silence descended over Heaven's courts.

When He spoke I could hear the incredible compassion and sorrow in the Father's voice.

"They will not fail Me."

"Beloved – My wisdom no longer resides in Satan as it used to in eons past.

"He is the father of lies – the destroyer – the thief.

"My omniscience has no place in him.

"Wisdom and understanding have long been replaced by cunning and all forms of guile.

"Truth by deceit.

"Goodness by unequivocal wickedness.

"His strategies against My children – against the elect, are short-sighted.

"He discounted one crucial element – that even the natural realm reflects the spiritual realm in that a *great test* foreshadows a *great promotion.*

"There was an allotted time to the great sifting, beloved.

"And so it began." Jesus' voice was very soft.

"For those whose lives had been sued, for it was a season of unspeakable, unbearable sorrow.

"The forces of hell and death, infirmity and tragedy were loosed as a tsunami against My Church.

"Carnage hit each of those lives whose Books of Life had been sued for by Satan.

"And the agonized cries of My Father's beloved –

"Of his most intimate saints – rose up to Him. Rose up before His Throne Room.

"And the cries grew stronger.

'Jesus, son of David, have mercy on me.'

'My God, my God, why have You forsaken me?'"

And the Father sat. Silent as the cries of His children's abandonment rose up before His throne.

Suddenly, I was back in the Father's chamber, sitting on His lap.

I hardly dared ask the question that burned in my soul.

Slowly I summoned up the courage to voice it –

"Did we all fail You, Father?"

I felt a single tear drop from the Father's eyes onto my face half buried in His chest.

He started to weep. The most precious sound in the entire universe.

"No, My child. My children did not fail Me.

"Yes, they screamed out in their sufferings.

"Yes, they clung to Me in utter desperation in their anguished night hours.

"Many felt completely abandoned by Me.

"But still, even in their utter anguish, pushed to the very brink of their ability to endure, I would hear them whisper, 'Daddy' and whisper, 'Jesus.'"

The Father looked down at my book of life.

"Even in the greatest times of your physical suffering when you did not want to live, when you felt you could not survive the hour, beloved, I saw your future.

"I saw this moment of you writing this book.

"I saw your present healing.

"I saw joy and hope spring back into your life.

"*You* could not see it, so overcome by the intensity of the sifting.

"But *I* saw this day.

"And I see the days of many, many reading this very book.

"I see their finest hour has yet to come."

"But, I was falling. I could only cling to you, Father."

"Yes. Such faith."

"Oh, no, Father; I failed you so badly."

Again, I felt the Father's smile and His great and tender pleasure.

"Beloved . . . ."

He was greatly moved.

"*In* those times of abandonment.

"*In* those times of utter desolation, when you felt completely abandoned by Me. And that Heaven was silent.

"When the lies of the enemy assailed your mind, screaming.

"When you clung to Me by what seemed to you to be just a thread.

"A gossamer thread.

"As some reading these pages are clinging right now.

"Know this, My child."

I watched as I saw the Father weeping.

"Your clinging to Me, My beloved child, was to Us one of the greatest acts of faith in your entire earthly life."

I was stunned.

Anyone who would have looked at me from the outside would have come to the conclusion I had no faith.

But, here in the Father's chamber, my Heavenly Father was telling me that it was in those moments of utter desperation, clinging only to Him by the most tenuous of threads.

That this was faith indeed.

I hung my head.

Day by day I had failed, sometimes terribly but always endured somehow by the grace of God till the next.

But I had never wept so many tears.

I had never been so assailed in my mind.

I had never come so close to having both my mind and my physical body and my spirit broken.

I felt an incredible wave of immense overwhelming love from my Father wash over me.

He spoke again.

"Courage is measured here in Heaven far differently than on Earth.

"When My children are hit by trials and testing that push them almost to the edge of their endurance.

"And yet still they stand

"Still they endure.

"Still they persevere.

"Still they believe.

"*That* is courage indeed.

MOREOVER [LET US ALSO BE FULL OF JOY NOW!] LET US EXULT AND TRIUMPH IN OUR TROUBLES AND REJOICE IN OUR SUFFERINGS,

KNOWING THAT PRESSURE AND AFFLICTION AND HARDSHIP PRODUCE PATIENT AND UNSWERVING ENDURANCE.

AND ENDURANCE (FORTITUDE) DEVELOPS MATURITY OF CHARACTER (APPROVED FAITH AND TRIED INTEGRITY). AND CHARACTER [OF THIS SORT] PRODUCES [THE HABIT OF] JOYFUL AND CONFIDENT HOPE OF ETERNAL SALVATION.

(Romans 5:3–4)

"Although you have won many battles and done many exploits through GOD TV and the media and will do many more – none, none of these exploits of faith come close to My heart. My so beloved child, to the times of the greatest trial you faced through infirmity, when you walked through the valley of the shadow and abandonment – pushed almost to the very boundaries of your endurance.

"And yet still you did not deny Me, *this* is when you won the over-comer's crown."

I could not even speak, I was so overcome by the Father's love.

I felt Him smile.

"Tell My children – be strong and of good courage for I have overcome the world."

Instantly, I was back in the courtroom.

And once again the High Courts of Heaven gathered.

One by one, the books of life were opened before the Father's throne.

I watched as I saw the Father's gavel pound down.

The words – 'Case dismissed' rang through the Heavenly High Courts.

Then I saw a bright, flaming, crimson liquid poured over every Book of Life that had been sued for.

And as it hit the books, it ignited into a fiercely burning flame.

Then I saw oil saturated with the Father's glory, poured over the Books and the most intense GLORY rose from their pages.

A great cry rang out from Satan, "The Trophy Rooms!"

SATAN'S TROPHY ROOMS – LEGAL PLUNDER

I was standing next to Jesus, staring into Satan's trophy rooms. They were so extensive that I could not see the end of the chambers.

The ceilings soared above me to an enormous height. They were cavernous, like great macabre museums.

They were strongly guarded, and each stolen treasure was fastened to the floor with great silver or gold manacles that seemed as though they were actually welded into the stone floors.

Satan strode into the trophy rooms.

He stood completely silent.

His eyes filled with unbridled rage.

At his nod, the heavy iron doors thundered shut.

Then I saw a strange, thick, black oily liquid oozing from the door frame. It appeared to be a sealant of some kind, and was now completely covering the doors. Satanic princes stood at each door to each chamber.

There was a blinding shaft of light.

Satan's expression transformed to fear. Then to terror.

I realized that we were standing in the trophy rooms where the trophies actually belonged to all those who had been sifted by the accuser in this past season.

Then the walls of the trophy room were saturated in the crimson blood of Jesus and the oil of glory.

The chamber shook and every manacle was instantly broken.

"He sifted them," Jesus said.

"His trophies, which were everything stolen from each of those sued for in this past season, are now legally My Father's property.

"And restitution demands sevenfold and more.

"The devil is legally bound to pay it."

I watched as huge manacles that held in place a huge casket that read, 'PHYSICAL HEALING; CREATIVE MIRACLES; FULL RECOVERY; HEALING FROM TRAUMA,' ruptured open.

Immediately, as the lid of the casket opened and, at the speed of light, body parts, brand-new physical kidneys, colons, hearts, livers, eyes, ears, brains, neurotransmitters, ovaries, pituitary glands, thyroids, stomachs, esophagi and throats, were dispatched to Earth by the angels.

I even saw whole new swathes of brand-new skin that was earmarked for one who had had a long and cruel battle with skin cancer, released down to Earth. I saw new hips and joints, all designated for those who had been sifted.

Then I saw shackles breaking off what seemed to be a huge treasury of gold and silver, oil, commodities, lands, houses, estates, all at lightning speed eject from the trophy room.

The Lord Jesus motioned to me to follow Him.

THE GOVERNMENTAL TROPHY ROOMS OF HELL

We travelled down.
     Down.
Down.

Until we passed through to another trophy room, more like a vast subterranean vault, guarded by huge, fierce satanic warriors with flaming swords.

This trophy room was so cavernous in size – it seemed like the size of a hundred Smithsonian museums put together.

Jesus and I started to walk, invisible to the guards, passing huge manacled trophies to our left and our right.

Each was manacled to the floor of the vault and guarded.

Jesus stopped. I followed His gaze upwards.

Soaring above us was a trophy the height of the Empire State Building.

"In this chamber you see the most highly prized of all of Satan's end-time trophies.

"These are the governmental spheres of influence on Earth, that belong to *Us*. That have been apprehended and stolen by the enemy for centuries.

"*This* is the financial realm."

Jesus moved His hand.

We stared ahead at what looked like a massive trading floor on Wall Street, except that it seemed to encompass every nation on Earth.

"This realm of finance will start to be repossessed and reclaimed by Our sons and daughters in these upcoming seasons on Earth.

"Many of the ones you saw sifted are now rising apostolically in the Earth with great authority and the spirit of might, legally mandated from Heaven's courts to destroy the enemy's hold over these trophies and transfer them back to My Father's Kingdom, that the great harvest may be financed and facilitated."

We continued walking.

"This is one you know well."

I stared up at the huge Hollywood sign above us.

"The entertainment industry," I mouthed.

Jesus nodded.

"It is yours for the taking.

"The Earth is about to see the greatest move of apostolic kingdom government overtake the spheres of finance, government, entertainment, media and communications.

"This is why the enemy fears the coming outpouring so violently.

"There is something else that you must see."

I followed Jesus' gaze straight ahead to what appeared to be another vast trading floor.

I studied it more closely. It was different from the trading floor that I had seen a few moments before. I could see thousands of battalions of demonic entities who seemed to be trading exactly as Earth's Wall Street does.

They were trading numbers.

And buying and selling.

But they were *buying* and *selling men's souls*.

I gasped, deeply shocked.

"Now watch closely," Jesus said softly.

I watched and suddenly saw the development of the movies *Chronicles of Brothers* announced on the demonic trading floor of souls.

Instantly, loud bells started to clang and pandemonium broke out over the floor. This was linked to the potential harvest of multiple millions, maybe even hundreds of millions of the unchurched, hearing the Gospel of Jesus Christ. The trading floor was inextricably linked to Satan's courtrooms.

Then I saw demonic legal scribes alerted in the courtrooms and my files and the files of our personal intercessor, who had faithfully prayed for Chronicles for years, were immediately called up and bought before a section of the enemy's court named 'Accusations of the Brethren.'

And they were added to the thousands and thousands of files piled up to the ceiling in a vault that read, 'Sued for Sifting.'

It was like a Department of Homeland blacklist.

Every one of those on the list had the potential to finance, usher in or equip multiple thousands and millions of the harvest.

But I was also completely aware that, although there would be a test, when it was over and passed – the outcome would be a legal decree in the Courts of Heaven that would be legally binding in the courts of the enemy.

Jesus watched as I took everything in.

Then He nodded.

THE THRONE ROOM – RESTITUTION

AND THE LORD BLESSED THE LATTER DAYS OF JOB MORE THAN HIS BEGINNING; FOR HE HAD 14,000 SHEEP, 6,000 CAMELS, 1,000 YOKE OF OXEN, AND 1,000 FEMALE DONKEYS.

HE HAD ALSO SEVEN SONS AND THREE DAUGHTERS.

AND HE CALLED THE NAME OF THE FIRST JEMIMAH, AND THE NAME OF THE SECOND KEZIAH, AND THE NAME OF THE THIRD KEREN-HAPPUCH.

AND IN ALL THE LAND THERE WERE NO WOMEN SO FAIR AS THE DAUGHTERS OF JOB, AND THEIR FATHER GAVE THEM INHERITANCE AMONG THEIR BROTHERS.

AFTER THIS, JOB LIVED 140 YEARS, AND SAW HIS SONS AND HIS SONS' SONS, EVEN TO FOUR GENERATIONS.

SO JOB DIED, AN OLD MAN AND FULL OF DAYS.

(Job 42:12–17)

We were back in the Throne Room.

I saw legions of the angelic hosts standing at attention.

On the altar was every man or woman who had experienced violent assault at the devil's hand.

It was time for restitution.

Some angels had healing vials in their hands.

Some held body parts.

Some held vials that said, 'Great peace, great joy.'

Some angels were holding gold, silver and treasures of wealth.

Some were holding title deeds to lost lands and houses.

Some held marriage certificates and, as the oil saturated these, broken fragments representing separation merged into a glorious white flame that rose in the shape of one united heart.

A great restoration of husbands and wives was about to fall on some of these.

And *then* the way was paved for a most glorious group of angels.

They walked straight before the Father.

Next to *each* angel was a man or a woman.

A boy or a girl.

And then I saw some angels holding babies in their arms.

And the Father said, "*These* are the ones that My children on Earth lost during this season.

"These are their husbands.

"Their wives.

"Their sons.

"Their daughters.

"Their babies."

And I *knew* as I watched the unfolding panorama, that this scene was specifically for all who read this book – these pages. Some of you have lost husbands, wives, sons and daughters in this past season.

"Tell them – tell My treasured, beloved children – that their loved ones are *with Me*.

"Tell them – that *not one* who was lost was a mistake.

"*Not one lost* was stolen by the enemy.

"I knew their time span on Earth was for this season.

"They did not come to Heaven early or out of time.

"*The way* they came was not from My hand or by My will – but their lives were not stolen from them.

"They are already teaching others.

"Preparing their loved ones' abodes.

"Fulfilling their eternal purpose.

"As with Job, I said that Satan could not take his life.

"These one's lives were always in My hands.

"And they are in My hands today."

And I saw an eight-year-old boy.

He was chatting with the Father *so* intimately.

Then the boy rose and I saw him teaching a great group of teenagers and young men with great authority.

And I knew that this was a baby who was recently lost by a prophet of God on Earth.

And here he was, already walking in his earthly father's mantle in Heaven in such great power, might and authority.

And now the preparation for My most glorious end-time move of healing throughout the entire Earth, the preparation for the mantle of My glory and My presence has begun."

I sank my head deeper into the Father's chest.

"And so, beloved, as their season of intense sifting and testing comes to an end. My sons and daughters.

"My dread champions are being raised from their sickbeds.

"Are being healed of their grief and bereavement.

"Are being delivered from their losses and their anguish.

"And, as they begin slowly but steadily to rise to a new day.

"Know this, My child – that Restitution is theirs, child.

"As it is yours.

"*Justice* is theirs, child.

"As it is yours.

"They will never be sifted again."

He hesitated.

"The great sifting is over.

"You are now off limits to Satan and your call is secured legally in the courts of Heaven.

"And now – prepare for the greatest visitation the Earth has ever seen.

Prepare for **Habitation** . . . ."

THE WORLDWIDE GLORY AND HEALING OUTPOURING

"*In* this present age, there has been the greatest unleashing of the spirits of infirmity and death against mankind from the satanic princes of hell. These spirits have not only been unleashed against My Church but against the whole of humanity."

Jesus grew quiet.

"Though My Church has suffered so greatly."

He turned to me, His face fierce.

"There has been a violent onslaught of infirmity against My children by the enemy in this past season. The enemy senses the mighty move of healing that is about to be released in power and might upon the Earth. Millions of My healing angels are preparing to come to Earth. Heaven's storehouses of healing are about to be emptied in the greatest, most powerful move of My healing hand that the Earth has ever seen. The enemy is terrified of this move and has been trying to preempt it by a violent assault of infirmity and sickness against My champions. To wear down the saints. To vex their spirits. And to break even My strongest warriors' minds.

"But the *tide is turning. The tide **is** turning.*

"And even those who have been so cruelly assigned in this past season shall begin to rise up with a supernatural strength. And I shall start to endow those who have stayed the course, no matter how weak they have been, they have still not denied My name. And you shall see those, the weak and infirm, shall start to strengthen their knees and shall rise up with a shout, 'I am strong!' And I shall endow the infirm with supernatural faith to be healed.

"And I shall pour out My Holy Spirit, the same Spirit who raised Me from the dead – upon them.

"And they shall rise from their wheelchairs.

"And they shall rise from their sickbeds.

"And even in an instant their minds shall be healed and sound.

"And a glorious shout – the shout of triumph – the sound of victory – shall erupt from these ones.

"Millions in My Body, our sons and daughters whom We love – who I laid My life down for on the cross are suffering great pain and their families great loss.

"I am coming.

"Many in My Church have lost hope – hope in My goodness, hope in My mercies, hope that I would heal *them* and, therefore, their faith has grown weak.

"Tell My children that My life was poured out, healing the sick and the desperate, when I walked the Earth and in *no manner* has that changed." Again I saw the fierce fire in His eyes.

"I came to destroy the works of the devil." Again He stopped and again His expression was fierce.

"To *obliterate* the works of the devil. The devil is running rampant through My Church. Many, many of My children are coming home prematurely. It is *not* the Father's will."

I hesitated because I knew that the Lord knew I did not want to write that sentence in the journal. I felt uneasy with it, but the Lord was not uneasy with it. He speaks plainly. He is truth.

"Tell My children that what I said in My Word is true. It stands. It stood 2,000 years ago when I walked the Earth. It stands today and it stands for the future. I am the Lord that healeth thee. All of these diseases I shall remove from you, for I am the Lord that healeth thee. Remember when I healed the little girl?"

I nodded. 'The girl who was dead?'

The Lord's eyes grew distant.

"Nothing is impossible with My Father." His face grew stern again. "Tell My children – *nothing* is impossible with My Father – *every* disease, every affliction, every cancer, every deaf ear and blind eye, if My children will only believe. And in the present state that My Church has entered into, faith is very weak, so we are raising up Our servants. We are raising up Our flames of fire and sending them throughout the Earth. You have seen a measure, even in this last season. But this is *just* the very beginning," said the Lord. "This is just the warm-up party."

And I saw Him soften and His eyes shone with that amazing humor He has.

"My child," His voice was earnest. "My Father and I are about to release the most powerful, unstoppable tsunami of healing and creative miracles from the windows of Heaven upon the Earth.

"Mighty flames of fire – called as healing evangelists in this last hour are rising. The dead will be raised, the blind will see, the deaf will hear, and AIDS and cancers healed will be commonplace.

"Resurrections will be commonplace."

The Lord looked at me to check my expression.

"*Commonplace*," He added emphatically.

"Kidneys will be created, new lungs transplanted from Heaven, hearts created, deformities will be healed, backs straightened, cripples will walk by the thousands in the arenas in the healing crusades of this last hour.

"And the healing anointing will not be confined to the evangelists, but there will be a great impartation of healing and creative miracles that will flow even to the very least of my brethren, and they shall go out into the highways and the byways and even as their shadow falls on the sick, so I tell you, My child, the sick shall be restored and healed.

"These are the things to come.

"I have sent this first wave and second wave in this present move to those of My own house primarily, that they may once again see miracles of the power and magnitude when I walked the Earth so that their faith may be restored and that they too might believe.

"Then I shall send them to the unbelievers. For indeed, My child, My Church at this present time is but a shadow of what it was in My time."

I winced, for I knew the power that so many of us lacked in our everyday walks. "But that will *change!*" And Jesus smiled.

THE DAY OF HABITATION

"For, oh, My child, how I yearn, how I yearn to live with My sons, to live with My daughters, to live with My children.

"For eons upon eons I have waited for this day.

"This day that comes swiftly upon the Earth.

"Let it not be said that it is only in the Millennium that I will come and live with My people.

"For I tell you that there draws near a different day.

"And a different season.

"And a different glory.

"For this different day is the day of Habitation.

"And I shall come as the Father.

"And I shall come as the Son.

"And I shall come as the Holy Spirit.

"And in the cloud I shall come.

"And in the fire I shall come.

"And in the glory I shall come.

"And in the cities I shall come.

"And in the slums I shall come.

"And to the lowly I will come.

"And to the wealthy I shall come.

"And to the self-sufficient I shall come.

"And to the needy and the hurting and the desperate I shall come.

"And it is in this day.

"In this day and in this hour of habitation that there shall be an overshadowing.

"An overshadowing of My presence."

"For this is not a visitation, this is not *just* a visitation.

"But, this is the day and the hour when I shall *dwell* with My people.

"This is the day and the hour when I shall *dwell* in My people.

"This is the day and the hour when not only shall My children abide in Me but they shall know that I abide in them.

"And their hearts shall be a habitation of My Spirit.

"And their homes shall be a habitation of My Spirit.

"And their schools shall be a habitation of My Spirit.

"And their workplaces shall be a habitation of My Spirit.

"And their streets shall be a habitation of My Spirit.

"And My presence shall overshadow towns and cities.

And even entire cities shall say, 'The Lord our God is with us.'

"And the darkness shall flee.

"And I shall make My place among you.

"Not only in the millennium shall it be. 'Oh, no,' says the Lord.

"But My sons and My daughters who have yearned for My presence.

"My sons and My daughters who have hungered for My touch.

"My sons and daughters who have yearned for My living waters upon their thirsty souls.

"They shall yet say there is a God.

"And He abides with me.

"'Habitation! Habitation! Habitation!' says the Living God

"*Prepare for the Day of Habitation.*"

RESTORATION – MY STORY

*B*eloved, there is nothing that I found when I was in the season of such adversity that gave me more hope than someone's testimony.

My greatest desire is that what is written next will give you such real hope.

My whole life that was lost has been restored. And in magnitude.

And I have received words that the restoration and justice haven't even hardly begun!

While I was sick, I desperately longed to live back in the Southwest of England, but in the natural it was completely impossible.

We owned our house in Kansas and even if we sold it, the UK housing market was so expensive that we could hardly get back on the property ladder.

But visionaries as we are, Rory found the most incredible Georgian country home only six miles from our studios in the Southwest.

But it was completely out of our reach financially.

While we were in Jerusalem, during my first shaky appearance back on TV, our beloved friend Kim Clement felt a strong word from the Lord that he and Jane were to give a gift towards our home in England that would be a 'provoking' gift that would 'provoke' others to give.

At this time, I was still sick and on my way to Bethel in Redding.

Well, a miracle was in process.

The property market in Kansas was still in a major slump, but we managed to sell our house in a period of about six weeks.

With the house sale and through the incredible generosity of two other amazing friends who responded to Kim and Jane's challenge by sowing several hundred thousand dollars into our family, we were able to procure a long-term lease on this most amazing home I had ever had in my life.

Beloved, you may say, well, that's because you are co-founders of GOD TV, but the truth is, as many in ministry will attest to, that in ministry, personal gifts both large and small are very rare, in fact, we had sowed our savings into GOD TV, trusting the Lord to stand in the gap for our family. Oh, and He did above and beyond anything we could have dreamed. This was a *miracle!*

I was still too sick to enjoy our home at first, but three years later, we live in the most incredible country home, beyond anything I could ever have dreamed.

Our dog and cat are with us, spoiled rotten and none the worse for wear!

Plus we have another Ridgeback. In fact, they are both in my office as I'm writing this, looking out of the window onto our beautiful walled English garden.

Our son and daughter are now young adults and are amazing!

I am back on TV, traveling back and forth to Israel and once again fully involved with my creative and programming teams.

I completed the fourth book in the Chronicles of Brothers series – *A Pale Horse* – and am presently writing the fifth book as well as designing the graphic novel of *Fall of Lucifer.*

My body is becoming stronger and stronger every day.

There are still seasons when I have to stand physically, but without fail, *every* area of my life that was ravaged by the enemy, has either been blessed beyond measure or is in the process of restoration and blessing.

The Father, the Son and His precious Holy Spirit have been so faithful to me and I just know that if you are presently walking that 'longest road,' that they are right in this season of your life standing in the gap for you – whispering, "Beloved son, beloved daughter, don't give up now – weary heart – for your best is yet to come!"

MY FATHER'S CHAMBER

"*D*addy . . . ," I snuggled into the chest of my Heavenly Father. "Our book is nearly finished . . . ."

We sat in beautiful silence.

I closed my eyes.

There was no place that I felt more safe or at home than on my Father's lap.

I sensed Him smile. I glanced up.

"But not quite . . . ."

He smiled tenderly.

There was a long silence.

"You want me to share about the golden letters?"

He nodded.

I slid off the Father's lap.

The golden letters were still there. Glistening, pure gold, almost hovering over what appeared to be an archaic scroll that lay on the table in front of us.

The word on the scroll was made up of nine letters, but only the first four were set in gold.

The word was 'Testimony.'

I looked back up at my Father.

"Tell My children, that there is never a testimony without first a TEST.

"And that there is always a test before a promotion," He said softly.

"The greater the test; the greater the promotion.

"Oh, tell My children not to give up, beloved.

"No matter how fierce the trial gets. Never give up.

"For like Daniel and Joseph, their test may prove to be the redemption, the deliverance of an entire marketplace.

"An entire nation.

"An entire generation.

"When Joseph was in the pit and the prison, if he could only have guessed what was ahead, if he could have seen the future – that his brothers' jealousy, Potiphar's wife's false accusations, the chief butler's 'amnesia' – every situation that seemed so out of his own control – that these were the exact circumstances – they were the exact tests that perfectly positioned him at the appointed time from heaven – to become the deliverer of Egypt."

The Father was now serious. Very serious.

"Many seeming injustices, betrayals, hardships, setbacks . . . .

"Many situations that seem in the natural world to be completely devastating and out of My children's control . . . .

"Some of the fiercest testing and trials that My children have been facing in this past season, are serving behind the scenes in the spirit realm as Heaven's vehicles for the greatest testimonies ever to break out across this Earth. If only My sons and My daughters don't give up under the intensity of the pressure of attack.

"And when the test is over, they will defeat the devil by the blood of My Son and the word of their TESTimony."

I looked up at the Father.

He was smiling broadly.

"My children are about to be promoted. And the whole of *hell cannot stop them.*

"For, I have overcome the world."

An all-consuming joy radiated from the Father's entire being.

"For I AM."

YOU KNOW HOW WE CALL THOSE BLESSED (HAPPY) WHO WERE STEADFAST [WHO ENDURED]. YOU HAVE HEARD OF THE ENDURANCE OF JOB, AND YOU HAVE SEEN THE LORD'S [PURPOSE AND HOW HE RICHLY BLESSED HIM IN THE] END, INASMUCH AS THE LORD IS FULL OF PITY AND COMPASSION AND TENDERNESS AND MERCY.

(James 5:11)

Other Books by Wendy Alec

Journal of the Unknown Prophet

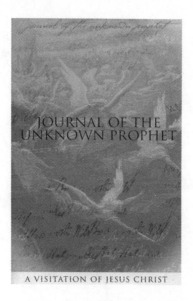

Wendy Alec's powerful book is a divine revelation of the Lord Jesus Christ and His cry for a deeper intimacy with each and every person on earth.

For the unbeliever, it represents a profound picture of who Jesus really is and how much He cares – how He has always been there for them, and how He wants to enrich their lives.

For the believer, it is an extraordinary challenge to walk in the fullness of everything God has in store for His beloved children.

Available now from your local book store or from Amazon and other on-line retailers.

www.wendyalec.co.uk
twitter: @wendy_alec

Chronicles of Brothers – Book 1

The Fall of Lucifer

Chronicles of Brothers – Book 2

Messiah: The First Judgement

Order now on

www.chroniclesofbrothers.com

or from Waterstones, Amazon, Barnes and Noble
or your local independent book store.

Join us on Facebook:
www.facebook.com/chroniclesofbrothers

Chronicles of Brothers – Book 3

Son of Perdition

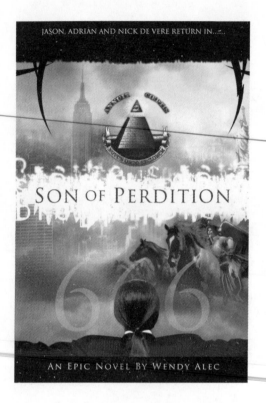

Order now on

www.chroniclesofbrothers.com

or from Waterstones, Amazon, Barnes and Noble
or your local independent book store.

Join us on Facebook:

www.facebook.com/chroniclesofbrothers

Chronicles of Brothers – Book 4

A Pale Horse

Order now on

www.chroniclesofbrothers.com

or from Waterstones, Amazon, Barnes and Noble
or your local independent book store.

Join us on Facebook::
www.facebook.com/chroniclesofbrothers

Wendy Alec, the author, was born in London, England.
Coming from a background in the arts and media,
she is the Programming and Creative Director of GOD TV,
a leading global religious broadcasting network
that she co-founded with her husband.

www.wendyalec.co.uk
twitter: @wendy_alec